The Smart Student's Guide to Healthy Living is a must for any parent sending their student off to college. The book is packed with practical tips for healthy eating. It helps answer the questions I hear from college students every day. This book is the answer to helping teens stay healthy and fit as they transcend the college years into adulthood. Hats off to M.J. and Fred Smith for giving students and easy-to-read survival guide to healthy eating at college.

> —Ann Blocker, RD, LD, CDE, director of nutrition at Veterans Memorial Hospital and nutrition consultant to Luther College, in Decorah, IA

A great book, so practical and useful—fantastic!

> —Jane Hasek, MSN, Ed.D., chancellor emerita and distinguished professor at Allen College in Waterloo, IA

I've lost another two pounds this week. I know that I'm losing it through exercise and diet. My stamina in exercising is increasing while my appetite is decreasing...I feel that I am working harder and longer without being any more tired. I really enjoy exercising and feel great doing it. My mood is better because I feel better about myself.

> —Andy Wannigman, student

I have been using the tips in the book and have a success story. I feel great! It's that plain and simple. I feel better about myself. I'll continue this plan next semester. I liked the results a lot and I hope to get more of the same the longer I participate...

—Dana Roberts, student

the
smart student's guide to healthy living

how to survive stress,
late nights & the college cafeteria

M.J. SMITH, RD, FADA • FRED SMITH

New Harbinger Publications, Inc.

Publisher's Note

This publication is designed to provide accurate and authoritative information in regard to the subject matter covered. It is sold with the understanding that the publisher is not engaged in rendering medical, psychological, financial, legal, or other professional services. If expert assistance or counseling is needed, the services of a competent professional should be sought.

Distributed in Canada by Raincoast Books.

Copyright © 2006 by M. J. Smith and Fred Smith
New Harbinger Publications, Inc.
5674 Shattuck Avenue
Oakland, CA 94609
www.newharbinger.com

Cover design by Amy Shoup; Text design by Amy Shoup and Michele Waters-Kermes; Acquired by Jess O'Brien

ISBN 1-57224-474-7 Paperback
Library of Congress Cataloging in Publication Data on file

08 07 06

10 9 8 7 6 5 4 3 2 1

First printing

Dedicated to Dad and Liz

Who, during the months we were writing this book, always believed it was a message that mattered.

contents

acknowledgments

A book of this scope, one intended to help students in dorm rooms all across the country, could not be written through one person's experiences. Rather, we needed many experiences— male and female, older and younger, those finishing college and others just starting down the road of academia. These people, who generously shared their experiences so that others might be enlightened, are as follows: Jonathan Thompson, Brian Lund, Ashley Thein, Jessica Moser, Lisa Krall, Christina Mick, Adam Teske, Ashley Hess, Emma Peterson, Sarah Kneller, Leah Kinnaird, Jamie Holmberg, and Annalise Conaway.

We needed additional students to field-test our work. For one month, they helped with a pilot study. They tested specific strategies that were rooted in the science of eating right, keeping fit, and managing stress. They ate salads before dinner, went to bed at the same time each night, or did a dorm room workout and shared commentary along the way. This group included Aaron Pyzdrowski, Rachel Appelt, Dana Roberts, Andrew Rindfleisch, Ben Pepin, Scott Boyken, Andrew Wannigman, Ben Moburg, and Joe Beatty.

A special thank-you goes to students Craig Finch, Chantel Olufsen, and Paul Beatty for putting up with Fred's panic attacks and for their moments of brilliance and their inherently positive attitude that the book would one day be printed.

The medical experts quoted in this book are not only longtime friends, but people we seek out when a doctor, dietitian, or physical therapist is needed. To Wayne, Mona, Geoff, and Carolyn, thanks.

Because we are privileged to count gifted writers among our friends, several came to our assistance during the copyediting phase. Thank you Drew Bahlmann, Julie Cull, and Jane Siebrecht.

As the book was finished, there were muses, agents, and editors who helped this work find its right publishing home. They are publisher David Wexler, editors Jeff Braun, Claire Lewis, and Heather Koshiol, author Cheryl Kimball, and agent Betsy Thorpe. Even at the eleventh hour, as the publishers calculated the market for this book, our cousin and marketing consultant Jane McCracken Murray and her husband Alex Murray chimed in with several nimble approaches.

And finally, to members of the incredible talent pool at New Harbinger, we appreciate your scrupulous attention to quality. These folks include Sarah Craft, who first noticed our manuscript, our editor Jess O'Brien, and Miriam Kleinerman, Troy DuFrene, Amy Shoup, Michele Waters, and Heather Mitchener.

science & tools
to do it yourself

It was the spring of 2004, and time for a freshman college student to nail down a summer job. My son, Fred Smith, who was finishing his first year at Luther College, had an idea. He wouldn't get a job. He'd write a book—with my help. It would be about eating right, keeping fit, and managing stress in college.

Fred had some important qualifications for this story. In the span of his first seven months away from home, he had gained weight, ditched his workout routine, and made an appointment with a counselor.

I had written over a dozen books on diet and nutrition topics, and after taking a big gulp and thinking, "You mean, you're going to turn down that job making calls for the mortgage company," I signed on to the partnership.

He would write in the basement and I would edit upstairs. We'd have our team meetings on the porch. At one of those first sit-down hammer-it-out sessions, we came up with a working title: *Take Mom to College*. After all, when students graduate and leave home, they say good-bye to the structure and encouragement that make eating right, keeping fit, and getting sleep a lot easier than it is in college.

But not long into the project, as we were talking to students and recording their struggles and aspirations for keeping a healthy balance in their new environment, I knew the working title didn't fit. It wasn't about relying on Mom or Dad at all.

The book was written with the realization that you—this new-century generation—can do it for yourselves. With the best science and tested tools, you can eat right, keep fit, get sleep, and stay organized. As an author and parent, the most important thing I have learned from Fred and all the students involved in this project is that you are our creative, industrious, and intelligent future.

—M. J. Smith MA, RD, FADA

I Wish I Had Had a Book Like This

I wish I had had a book like this when I started college. I wish I had had a book like this when I began my journey to independence—a book with instructions for what to do about a rubber-band waistline, an increased stress load, an erratic schedule, and a novice ability to manage my time. Upon graduation from high school, I was a fit, competent eighteen-year-old with a why-not attitude. Nothing was going to stop me from taking freshman year by storm. Little did I know that over the course of the next year, I was to gain and lose weight many times. I was to struggle through periods of feeling baffled about how to do it all. By the end of freshman year, I looked in the mirror and knew I needed help. So I decided to write the book I needed.

As a dietitian who's written over ten books on healthy eating and a recognized fellow of the American Dietetic Association, my mom, M. J. Smith, was in a perfect position to help me put things in perspective. She told me that though much has changed since she was in college in the 1970s, when it comes to food and stress, college students struggled with the same issues back then. She agreed to write this book with me and bring her dietetic expertise to bear.

We knew that we could not write this book as a duo, so we enlisted the help of other college freshmen and experts in the fields of nutrition and college health services and counseling. What we learned from them became the basis for the pages beyond this introduction. Over the course of one summer, we obtained firsthand reports and reflections from students who had survived their first year on their own. These students spoke sincerely and informatively. Their insights drew a picture of young people learning about lifestyle challenges and coping strategies. We then consulted with the experts. Because fitness, sleep, and stress are all related to well-being, we also consulted with Dr. Wayne Kelly, a physician who had twenty years experience in Health Services at Winona State College. We also consulted with Geoff Twohill, a therapist at Yale-New Haven Hospital, who works with undergraduate students.

Here we've put together the best of what all these experts have to offer. Now, instead of entering college without the tools to successfully take charge of food, fitness, and stress, you can use our research as practical advice.

I wish I had had this book ... and I am glad you do now.

—*Fred Smith*

introduction

Have college students always experienced sleep deprivation, weight gain, and general malaise? Probably so, but it doesn't have to be that way. This book will help you be the exception. Here's what to expect:

The best answers to common problems, presented in a ready-reference format. Need a cold remedy, like Chicken Soup in the Dorm? Wondering about what zinc really does for the body? Looking for cheap and healthy ways to manage stress? Concerned about your roommate's unusual exercise pattern? The answers are all here. It isn't point and click, but it's almost as fast. Call it turn and scan. Most college students grow to hate thick textbooks with small print, thin pages, and zero dialog. Therefore, this user-friendly resource guide does not fit that description. It is a reference for information that you may want to return to from time to time. Place it on your bookshelf within easy reach so you can pull it down when you feel fat, fatigued, or sluggish. It is a book to turn to when you know it is time to take better care of yourself and you want to read the testimonials from students just like you.

This book is so much more than a diet plan. It deals with everything from an ABC rating of college cafeteria food to a powerful six-minute workout, to recommendations on pillows. If you want to go directly to avoiding "the freshman fifteen," turn to chapter 1. Struggling and stressing out over time management? We've got tips in chapter 7, How to Stay Organized (since mom isn't there to remind you how). And if you want to turn your dorm into a sanctuary where you can relax, breathe deeply, and learn, check out chapter 5, on sleep. Chapter 4 covers keeping fit, and chapter 6 is on healthy ways to release stress.

The strategies were tested by students just like you. When the book was drafted, college students actually tested its strategies for three weeks. They tried out the strategies for healthy eating, keeping fit, getting sleep, managing stress, and staying organized, and they recorded journal entries about their experiences. These real-life reports show up throughout the book and guided its final editing.

So, right here on these pages, you have real-life advice that has been proven to work. But ultimately, no one can tell you how to do everything, and you will certainly come up with improvements on our ideas. Go ahead, write in the margins. One thing this book will not do is chastise you for decisions you make. This is a guide to healthy eating, healthy living, and excelling in college. If you're naturally more productive watching television and eating popcorn while you study, congratulations! But if you struggle with motivation to exercise, consider chapter 4 the next best thing to a personal trainer. The point is, we are here to help. Undoubtedly, as a college student living away from the hands-on support of home and family, you have many questions. Here are just a few of the important ones our book will answer for you:

- When, what, and where do I eat to perform at my best cognitive level?

- How can I make ten minutes count toward fitness?
- How much sleep do I need, and how can I get it?
- How do I deal with my new priorities and still make time for myself?

Begin. Turn the page. Learn two simple ways to begin eating right.

two different food plans to avoid the freshman fifteen

It's not an urban myth. We all know this notion of the "freshman fifteen" came from a college somewhere. The freshmen we interviewed for this book were no different. It turns out that if you don't follow a plan for eating healthy, you will get used to your jeans feeling tighter and tighter.

Weight gain, even a few pounds, makes people feel just plain uncomfortable. But in college, if you aren't careful, before you know it you'll be freaked out by the number on the scale. That is exactly what Cornell University Nutrition Science professor David Levitsky found. His 2004 study of sixty freshman students concluded, "Significant weight gain during the first semester of college is a real phenomenon" (Lang 2003). Freshmen enrolled in his scientific trial gained 0.3 pounds per week, on average. That is just plain scary. Levitsky cited the all-you-can-eat dining facilities, late evening snacks, weekend meals, and junk food as significant predictors of weight gain (Levitsky and Youn 2004). This professor's research confirms that college weight gain comes from a relatively small increase in calories each day or week, but the cumulative effect is not a small matter. It is extra pounds and inches that most of us don't need or want. What's more, it *is* a challenge to eat both cheaply and healthfully, especially in a dorm room.

This book is going to show you how you can.

We know you're not always able to eat at the same time every day. But with a list of healthy snacks and an ABC rating of cafeteria food, you'll soon know how to get all the nutrition you need from foods you like, in spite of your demanding schedule of courses, music lessons, and work-study. It will take some effort on your part, but like a favorite family recipe, this is a formula that works. So, if you're up for the challenge, continue reading! Now it's your turn to get serious about eating right and get the best advice for avoiding the freshman fifteen in college.

No one really has time to keep track of calories or count carbohydrates in college, so this chapter begins with two different but simple methods for you to maximize nutrition for brainpower and weight control.

In this chapter, you will quickly learn two distinct ways to think about eating. The first is choosing whole and colored foods and limiting refined foods. This system is based on the idea of evaluating food choices and then placing the items in one of two categories. Nutrients like vitamin C, iron, and zinc abound in whole and colored foods. This is what makes them healthy. These essential food chemicals are less concentrated and harder to find in refined foods. Using our simple lists will help you select whole and colored food choices easily. Think of it as a form of comparison shopping as you walk through the hot food line in the café or deli aisle of the grocery store. You'll be shopping for the best nutrient value for the least number of calories.

The second food plan is a straightforward ABC grading of cafeteria foods. With this plan, you simply refer to a list and select A and B choices most of the time. You'll still have to think with this plan, because with all the jazzy combinations of menu items in your cafeteria, you'll have to find the item most like it on your ABC lists. Students who tested both the whole and colored foods plan and the ABC plan actually photocopied lists from the book and kept the lists in their billfold or backpack. Both plans work. It is up to you to decide which works best for you.

Let's start with the first food plan. It's a simple concept that can be remembered in a simple sentence whether you're at the cafeteria salad station or in a restaurant.

Choose Whole & Colored Foods & Limit Refined Foods

Let's start with the *limit* part of this food plan.

WHY YOU WANT TO LIMIT REFINED FOODS

Refined white flour and sugar are the kind of simple carbohydrates that rev up your insulin production and your appetite. This is based on a scientific measure called the *glycemic index*. When you eat a handful of chocolate chip cookies (cookies contain both flour and sugar, if you remember that Toll House recipe you made with your grandma), sugar is delivered lickety-split to your blood. Insulin production goes into overdrive as it is called up to deliver the sugar or glucose to your cells. When insulin's job is done, your blood sugar level drops and you feel hungry again. So you eat another cookie, knowing you're not really hungry. The other problem with sugar and refined flour concerns what they are missing. While they provide calories from carbohydrates, they contribute few other vital nutrients—no protein to rebuild brain cells, and not a trace of vitamin C to fight colds and flu. So, foods laced with sugar and white flour should be a low priority when dining in the cafeteria.

Now comes the best part of this food plan.

CHOOSE WHOLE & COLORED FOODS

No guilt, no second-guessing. We know it sounds too simple to really work. But a whole foods approach to eating is used by the most successful national weight-control programs. This system may be your preference because you can master the concept in your head in these four words: eat whole/limit refined. Using this plan will help you eat whole and colored foods and keep your diet as free of white flour and sugar as possible.

You will learn to appreciate foods for being "closest to the vine." Let's use apples as an example. A fresh apple is on the whole and colored list. No-sugar-added applesauce is on the whole list because it's free of added sugar. Sugar-free apple cider is also a good choice. Sweetened applesauce, apple fritters, and apple cake are on the list to be limited because they contain sugar and flour.

Here is another way to think about whole and colored foods. Look at the salad bar. Lined up in neat rows, you see pasta salad, coleslaw, melon balls, romaine lettuce, cherry tomatoes, croutons, and bacon bits. Now ask yourself, "How close are these foods to how they were grown?" Choose foods closest to their original form: melon balls, romaine lettuce, and cherry tomatoes. The melon has been peeled and cut into cute little balls, but the lettuce and tomatoes don't appear much different on the salad bar than they did in the garden. In other words, these whole foods go onto your salad plate first. The pasta is made from white flour, salt, and water. White pasta is highly processed and bears little resemblance to whole grain wheat, and refined white flour is not exactly vital to support life. Let the pasta salad go. Coleslaw—well, the cabbage is close to the vine. So that is good. But the sweet, slick dressing may be full of sugar. Settle for a small spoonful of coleslaw.

Choosing whole and colored foods is the most natural and most healthy way to think about food, because vitamins and minerals and micronutrients are removed at every step of food processing.

Beyond providing a vitamin- and mineral-rich diet, eating whole and colored foods is a sure way to boost dietary fiber intake. This nutrient, which is nondigestible, provides a natural packaging and structure to foods, like the skin on a potato or the strings in celery. Fiber is now widely recognized by dietitians as an aid to weight control. Counting grams of dietary fiber is part of successful and respected national weight-loss plans like Weight Watchers. A study conducted at the University of Hawaii by Dr. Nancy Howarth looked at twenty-year-old adults and their intake of dietary fiber. Dr. Howarth found that, especially for women, boosting fiber intake was more effective than controlling fat as a singular strategy for weight control. Taken together, a high-fiber, low-fat diet was most effective (Howarth et al. 2005).

What is it about fiber that promotes a healthy weight? Dr. Howarth suggests two factors. A high-fiber diet is less energy dense. In other words, a high-fiber meal takes up more space and contains fewer calories. Second, there is a slower absorption of energy and a longer-lasting sense of fullness after a high-fiber meal. Use the lists below to select whole and colored foods that are high in fiber at each of your meals and snacks.

Choose Whole & Colored Foods
Higher in Fiber

- Brown rice
- 100 percent wheat bread
- Wheat tortillas
- Squash
- Fresh peaches
- Whole wheat crackers
- Smoked almonds
- Whole grain cereal with raisins
- Raspberry smoothie with yogurt
- Strawberries
- High-pulp orange juice
- Whole fresh apple

Limit Refined Foods
Lower in Fiber

- White Rice
- White Bread
- White Tortillas
- Dumplings
- Sugar Cookies
- White corn chips
- Potato chips
- Pancakes
- Ice cream
- Strawberry cake
- Orange soda
- Apple fritter

What About Sugar?

Maybe you went through high school too busy to read or ever wonder about food labels. Maybe you find yourself, for the first time, really seriously wondering how to eat right. If so, here are some foods that are high in sugar:

- Sherbet
- Frozen dairy desserts
- Pie
- Cheesecake
- Pudding
- Chocolate candies
- Hard candy
- Sweetened fruit drinks
- All cookies
- Cake
- Cupcakes
- Brownies and bars
- Custard
- Candy bars
- Sweetened coffee drinks
- Sodas

It might seem like the list of sugary foods is pretty long. It also contains a lot of familiar foods. Remember, we suggested that you limit refined foods. This means that when there is a more nutritious and natural choice available that you enjoy, avoid or limit foods with sugar and white flour. One whole food choice at a time leads to one healthy meal, then one good day, followed by one slim week, leading to a month when you look and feel great. Every single intelligent choice you make will add up. Even making three whole food choices and one refined food choice at a meal is a success if you have never approached eating in this way before. Soon, you will know and love the whole and natural eating style. Here are some other colored whole foods that you probably already like:

- All fresh vegetables, including carrots, cauliflower, radishes, celery, cherry tomatoes
- All canned and frozen vegetables
- Tomato or V8 juice
- All fresh fruits, including bananas, grapes, bing cherries, pears, pineapple

- All 100 percent fruit juices
- All frozen fruit and canned fruit in juice
- Broiled or grilled chicken or fish
- Broiled or grilled beef or pork
- Roast beef, chicken, and pork
- Canned or packaged tuna, salmon, or sardines
- Canned chicken
- Oil and vinegar salad dressing
- Olive oil
- All fresh greens and green salads, including spinach salads, Caesar salads with chicken and shrimp, Cobb salads, Greek salads, club salads
- All broth-based soups with vegetables
- Whole wheat bread, buns, and bagels
- Whole grains like bran cereal, cracked wheat, and couscous
- Dried beans and peas, like black beans and refried beans
- Cheese, cottage cheese, and plain yogurt
- Skim and 1 percent milk (rather than 2 percent or whole)
- All nuts unless they are sugared
- Canola margarine (nonhydrogenated)

what students said:

Pete, a biology major from Minnesota, who tested the whole and colored foods plan: *I guess I view moderation as the first step to success when it comes to this diet. I am sticking with the no refined foods and eating the colored foods diet. I have three meals a day. I have avoided soft drinks entirely. My breakfast is usually a banana, cereal, and milk and then wheat toast. Although I have been eating healthy, I find myself having a random snack about every other day, whether it is a cookie or a mocha. But these have been in moderation. Most of all, I have found myself having more energy since I switched to this diet. I think I am even getting fewer headaches than normal.*

David, a political science major from Iowa: *When I first signed up for the whole and colored foods plan, I knew it was going to be hard to do, to eat the right foods in the cafeteria and to remember to do it every day. But when I read into it, this diet became easier to understand. You just eat less white bread and white pasta. Eating more veggies has become easier. After eating them at every meal, they begin to grow on you.*

Chris, a music major from South Dakota: *This diet is going great. I have never felt like I have eaten so well without destroying myself. I was very pleased to see that I have lost five pounds. I know that isn't much, but I realize this is a long process. I feel very comfortable being able to continue this diet for a long time.*

In addition to choosing familiar whole foods and discovering new ones, you may use condiments and beverages to complete your menu. The following foods are not particularly famous for their nutrient content, but are fine to use in moderation:

- Sugar-free yogurt
- Reduced-fat salad dressings
- Light cream cheese
- Light sour cream
- Condiments such as mustard, soy sauce, salsa, and ketchup
- Diet soda
- Sugar-free fruit drinks (such as sugar-free lemonade)
- Tea
- Coffee
  Note: A reasonable limit for tea and coffee with caffeine is four servings daily

The A, B, & C Cafeteria Choices

A second way for you to understand the benefits of whole and colored foods is by giving common cafeteria menu items a letter grade. They are organized into the following A, B, and C lists according to their nutrient qualities. No more guessing if the grilled chicken wrap is good for you. Turn to the A list and find it there when a whole grain tortilla is used. The A list includes common cafeteria foods highest in fiber, vitamins, and minerals and lowest in saturated fat, refined flour, and sugar. Selecting foods from the A list most of the time will help ensure you have the energy needed for optimal physical and mental performance. The B list includes foods that contribute less fiber, fewer vitamins, and minerals, and more fat, sugar, or refined flour. They may be selected from time to time. The C list includes foods that, calorie for calorie, provide fewer nutritional benefits and should be your last choice. You will find pancakes with syrup on the C list, but pancakes with fruit topping are on the B list. This grading scale is more sensitive to the fat content of a food than the simpler whole and colored food plan. As an example, lean breakfast ham gets an A, but bacon and sausage rate a C.

On the lists you'll see a suggestion that sugar-free soft drinks and coffee and tea be limited. This is because other beverages, like milk and 100 percent fruit and

Brandon, a music major from Minnesota, who tested the ABC plan for three weeks: *The ABC ratings have been a good guide to help me know what I should and shouldn't be eating. It's getting easier to choose healthy foods and I feel better from eating healthy, which is really nice.*

Darius, a political science major from Wisconsin: *I kept to this plan of eating lots of fruits and sticking to wheat bread. I have lowered my carb intake and concentrated on finding the good meats. Sometimes the meats in the cafeteria have a lot of fat and this requires me to find alternatives, like a sub sandwich. This diet has been good for me because it makes me more aware of what I eat. This diet gives me more energy, but it also requires me to eat more volume at mealtimes.*

vegetable juices, provide vital calcium, vitamin D, vitamin A, and vitamin C. They are better choices.

The grades are based on nutrient analyses of menus by Ramona "Mona" Milius, RD, director of Dining Services at the University of Northern Iowa. We also reviewed menus at the University of Iowa, Stanford University, Kirkwood Community College, Luther College, Iowa State University, Lake Superior College, University of Richmond, Illinois Central College, and Oklahoma City Community College to produce the ABC grading lists.

Which Plan Is Right for You?

Now you have been introduced to two new and easy ways to think about eating: the whole and colored food plan and the ABC cafeteria choices.

Thinking about whether a food is whole and unrefined is a concept that will take time to master, but you can do it in less than a week. Take the difference between a baked potato, mashed potatoes, and potato chips. The baked potato is still whole. The mashed potatoes, mixed with butter and milk, have lost their skins. The chips have been sliced and fried in oil. So use your intuition when comparing foods, and choose less refined for more nutrition and fewer calories.

If you would rather know for sure that your diet is grade A, then the second food plan may be better for you. You may appreciate knowing for sure that whole wheat toast is on the A list and that a whole grain muffin is on the B list (because it has sugar). But with either approach, you must be aware of four more planning issues. Let's look at portion size first.

The A List at Breakfast

- Low-fat and fat-free yogurt (with less than 20 grams of carbohydrate per cup)
- Whole grain cereal
- Bran or wheat flakes with fruit
- Oatmeal
- 100 percent whole wheat toast
- 100 percent whole wheat bagels (with non-hydrogenated canola oil margarine and jelly)
- Scrambled eggs
- Huevos rancheros
- Boiled eggs
- Hash brown potatoes with skins
- Veggie omelet
- Canadian bacon
- Whole fresh fruit
- Fresh fruit cup
- Grapefruit sections
- 100 percent fruit juice
- Skim or 1 percent milk

The B List at Breakfast

- Bran and whole grain muffins
- White bagels or white toast (with non-hydrogenated canola oil margarine and jelly)
- Cream of Wheat
- Pancakes or waffles with fresh fruit topping
- Yogurt with more than 20 grams of carbohydrate per cup
- 2 percent milk
- Egg bake with vegetables and/or ham
- Breakfast bagel sandwich with Canadian bacon or ham
- Hash browns
- Grits

The C List at Breakfast

- All muffins except bran and whole wheat
- White bagels with sugary toppings
- Fried eggs
- Egg bake with sausage or bacon
- Hash brown squares
- Caramel pecan rolls
- Frosted cinnamon rolls
- Pancakes or waffles with syrup
- Sausage links
- Sausage nuggets
- Crumb cakes
- Bacon
- Biscuits and gravy
- Doughnuts
- Fritters
- Biscuit or bagel breakfast sandwiches with sausage or bacon

The A List for Soups

- Chicken vegetable
- Vegetable beef
- Lentil
- Minestrone
- French onion
- Bean
- Split pea
- Vegetable barley
- Vegetable
- Roasted tomato
- Chicken and mushroom with rice
- Chili
- Black bean

The B List for Soups

- Chicken and dumpling
- Chicken and noodle
- Clam chowder
- Cheesy broccoli
- Potato
- Cream of corn

The C List for Soups

- Reuben chowder
- Cream-based soups

The A List for Sandwiches

- Wheat or whole grain breads
- Grilled chicken
- Grilled mushroom and vegetable
- Grilled pork tenderloin
- Vegetarian burger
- Turkey broccoli wrap
- Lean cold cut meats

The B List for Sandwiches

- For all sandwiches, request light mayo
- Barbecued beef
- Barbecued pork
- Crab melt
- Tuna or crab salad
- Chicken salad
- Ham salad
- Roast beef salad
- Egg salad

The C List for Sandwiches

- Italian chicken wing
- Reuben
- Cheeseburger
- Breaded fish
- Breaded chicken fillet
- Hog dog
- Bratwurst

17

The A List for Entrées

- Chicken and vegetable wrap (whole grain wrap)
- Whole wheat tortilla with chicken or bean filling
- Whole wheat pasta with red sauce and vegetables or chicken
- Beef pepper steak
- Grilled turkey tenderloin
- Roast pork cutlet
- Grilled shrimp
- Broiled cod or whitefish
- Shrimp, vegetables, and brown rice
- Whole wheat pizza
- Whole wheat lasagna
- Tofu and vegetables over fried rice
- Eggplant Parmesan
- Stuffed peppers
- Shrimp or crab and fresh vegetable salad
- Chinese chicken salad

The B List for Entrées

- Taco salad
- Tacos with bean or chicken filling
- Grilled chicken salad with cheese, vegetables, and greens
- Grilled chicken tenders
- Scalloped potatoes and ham
- White pasta with red sauce and vegetables or chicken
- Meat loaf
- Pork with barbecue sauce
- Chicken-fried steak
- Glazed ham
- Vegetarian lasagna
- Vegetarian pizza or Canadian bacon pizza

The C List for Entrées

- Deep-fried chicken, fish or shrimp
- Deep-fried pork tenderloin
- Chicken nuggets
- Chicken cordon bleu
- Chicken Parmesan
- Tater tot casserole
- Macaroni and cheese
- Tacos with beef filling
- Nachos with cheese and ground beef
- Creamy chicken casseroles
- White pasta and meat dishes
- Pasta with Alfredo sauce
- Pizza with sausage, beef, or pepperoni
- Calzones

Fruits and Vegetables Are All on the *A* List

- Carrots
- Green beans
- Spinach
- Broccoli
- Cauliflower
- Celery
- Zucchini
- Summer squash
- Tomatoes

- Peppers
- Peas and carrots
- Peas and pearl onions
- Roasted vegetables
- Mixed vegetables
- Corn
- Squash
- Apples
- Oranges

- Bananas
- Grapes
- Melons
- Pears
- Pineapple
- Peaches
- Apricots
- Mixed fruit cocktail without juice
- Grapefruit

The *A* List for Salads

- Choose clear (oil-based) or reduced-fat dressings
- Dark leafy green salad with fresh vegetables
- Coleslaw
- Three-bean salad
- Fresh marinated tomato salad
- Cucumber salads
- Carrot salads
- Fresh fruit salad without the syrup
- Sugar-free gelatin and fruit

The *B* List for Salads

- Fruit salads with syrup
- White pasta and vegetable salad with clear (oil-based) dressing
- White rice salads
- Sweetened gelatin salads with fruit

The *C* List for Salads

- Potato salad

The A List for Side Dishes

- Brown rice dishes
- Brown rice pilaf
- Baked potatoes with skins
- Refried beans
- Whole wheat pasta
- Baked beans
- Hummus and pita bread
- Black bean dishes
- Couscous

The B List for Side Dishes

- Creamed vegetables
- Vegetables with cheese sauce
- Mashed potatoes
- Spanish rice with vegetables made with white rice
- White rice pilaf

The C List for Side Dishes

- White pasta dishes
- Cheesy white rice dishes
- Au gratin potatoes
- Tater wedges or squares
- Nachos
- Cheese and white flour quesadillas
- Deep-fried cheese balls, mushrooms, cauliflower, or broccoli
- French fries

The A List for Beverages

- Skim or 1 percent milk for all milk
- 100 percent fruit juices
- Sugar-free chocolate milk
- Mineral water
- Sugar-free flavored water
- Sugar-free soft drinks
- Tea and coffee (one to four servings per day)
- Sugar-free iced tea
- Caffe latte—espresso with steamed milk
- Café au lait—equal portions of coffee and scalded milk
- Cappuccino—espresso with steamed milk foam

The B List for Beverages

- Fruit juice blends (such as Sunny Delight)
- Café mocha—espresso with chocolate syrup with steamed milk foam (with skim or 1 percent milk)
- 2 percent milk

The C List for Beverages

- Soft drinks
- Juice drinks
- Sweetened iced tea
- Whole milk
- Chocolate milk (unless sugar free)

The A List for Desserts

- Fresh fruit
- Unsweetened frozen fruit
- Canned fruit in juice
- Sugar-free ice cream or yogurt
- Sugar-free frozen yogurt
- Sugar-free frozen novelties—like frozen fudge bars

The B List for Desserts

- Small soft-serve ice cream or frozen yogurt
- Small serving of sherbet
- Angel food cake
- Oatmeal raisin cookies
- Pudding

The C List for Desserts

- Frosted cake
- Fruit crisp
- Cobbler
- Bread pudding
- Pie
- Cheesecake
- Regular ice cream
- Chocolate chip cookies
- Sugar cookies
- All other cookies
- Sundaes, malts, and shakes

The A List for Condiments

- Cocktail sauce
- Horseradish
- Hot sauce
- Ketchup
- Lemon or lime juice

- Mustard
- Salsa
- Soy sauce
- Steak sauce
- Sugar substitutes

- Taco sauce
- Teriyaki sauce
- Vinegar
- Worcestershire sauce

GAUGING PORTION SIZE

You have heard it from dietitians and weight-control counselors before: "Eat slowly and stop before you are pleasantly full." It would be great if we could take all the time in the world to eat. But in college this is an especially ridiculous expectation, because you usually have only a few minutes to grab lunch. However, you can still observe portion sizes.

- *For plain meat entrées* like hamburgers and grilled chicken, three ounces is the recommended portion. It is about the size of a deck of cards. Active college students may choose four to six ounces at a meal. So that would be up to two decks of cards.
- *For vegetables* it isn't really necessary to worry about eating too much broccoli, fresh spinach, or most other vegetables. But for starchy vegetables like squash, corn, and baked potatoes, stick with a cup. That is the size of a tennis ball.
- *For fruits* a cup size is again appropriate.
- *For grains* like brown rice and couscous and dried beans, again aim for one cup.
- *For whole wheat bread or tortillas,* start with one or two servings per meal.
- *For milk,* you still need three or four cups (up to a quart) a day, or the equivalent in calcium-rich dairy products like sugar-free yogurt, cheese, or low fat cottage cheese. Because most hard and creamy cheeses contain saturated fat, limit them to two or three ounces, two or three times a week. Choose reduced-fat or light cheese whenever possible.

ARE YOU HUNGRY, THIRSTY, FULL, OR JUST BORED?

Being aware of portion size is a good start to balancing your food intake with your energy needs. But to use either of these two eating plans wisely, you will need to eat when you are hungry, and not hold out until later. Likewise, you will have to learn to stop eating when you are satisfied. Either of these approaches allows you to eat as much as you need to feel satisfied. Consider the following hunger scale:

Starving	Want to Eat Now	Getting Hungry	**Comfortable**	Full	Too Full Feel Sick

When you think about food, the idea is to be aware of where you are on the hunger scale. If you are comfortable, it is not time to eat. If you are starting to get hungry and this is the only half hour slot you have for lunch, then go ahead and eat something light. If you feel like you want to eat now, your hunger is acute. Be as thoughtful as you can to select something from the A list. If you are starving, well, it is not easy to think through your food selections.

As you eat, be aware of how you move on the hunger scale: from hungry to comfortable to full. Stop before you feel full, or you will move to the uncomfortable place of being too full. Feeling stuffed, with your waistband pressing into your skin, is a negative message you will associate with eating, and a food-related stress you can avoid by pushing back your plate, folding up your napkin, and stopping. Do this before you feel sick.

Keep in mind that thirst is often confused for hunger. If you are thinking about nibbling on something, ask yourself if a glass of ice-cold water would be satisfying. Drink it. Then wait fifteen minutes. Thirst mechanisms are different from hunger mechanisms. It is easy to confuse the two, so answer first with a glass of water.

IT'S ALL ABOUT PLANNING AHEAD

Ramona "Mona" Milius has been feeding thousands of college students for over twenty years at the University of Northern Iowa. Currently, as president of the National Association of College and University Food Services, she leads the nation in the art and science of making meals that college students will love. She has planned and supervised the construction and renovation of three state-of-the-art dining plazas where students nibble on personalized stir-fry combinations, slurp fruity smoothies, and chew on stone-hearth pizzas. When Mona was interviewed for this book, she kept coming back to a universal problem she has observed among students: lack of meal planning.

The first step is just to plan when in your busy day you are going to find time to eat. Mona observed, "Students will walk all the way across campus for a great place to eat" (Milius 2004). So, build your daily class and work schedule with time for snack and meal breaks.

DON'T BLOW OFF BREAKFAST

There is a reason breakfast is served in public schools. Numerous studies (Kleinman 2002) have documented the positive relationship between eating a nutritious breakfast and increased educational achievement. The reverse of this is true as well. Students who begin their school day without breakfast demonstrate a steady decline in attention in the late morning hours, a negative attitude, and a drop in scholastic achievement. Growling stomachs are more than just a distraction from the learning process. Skipping breakfast affects the ability to focus and the speed and accuracy of problem-solving tasks.

Not only does breakfast promote learning retention, research shows that eating breakfast plays a part in successful weight control. Almost 80 percent of people who successfully control their weight chow down on this meal (American Heart Association 2003). Think of breakfast as the sparkplug for your body's engine.

Your metabolism slows as you sleep, and the process of digesting food speeds it up again. Early morning nutrients also provide energy for early morning activity. Finally, you should know that along with this energy comes vitamins and minerals. Overall, people who eat a well balanced breakfast tend to have more nutritious diets than those who skip it (Rampersaud et al. 2005).

This means, for example, that if your breakfast habit consistently includes a food or juice rich in vitamin C, like fresh strawberries or grapefruit juice, your morning routine will add up to fewer colds and flus.

A recent review of forty-seven different nutrition studies corroborated the benefits of breakfast for preventing disease and maintaining weight. This review, conducted by registered dietitian Gail Rampersaud and colleagues at the University of Florida (2005), led to these conclusions:

- Breakfast significantly contributes to whole diet nutrient adequacy.
- Breakfast consumers are likely to have better overall fiber intake.
- Breakfast consumption benefits cognitive function, particularly memory, academic performance, psychosocial function, and mood.
- Breakfast may also reduce the risk of diabetes, because those who skip the morning meal are more than four times as likely to be obese as people who eat breakfast regularly.

Once you've mastered the breakfast routine, don't wait until three o'clock to think about lunch. If you do, you'll be feeling so cranky and shaky that you'll eat anything nearby, even if it's unhealthy, just to stop your stomach from growling. Figure out just when you're going to be able to get to the cafeteria. Then, as you march up the steps hungry as a bear, take a few seconds to answer these questions: What I am hungry for? And will my choices energize me for the work ahead? Use the following list to plan what goes on your tray:

- A *protein food* such as eggs, beans or peas, cheese, meat, fish, or poultry, to regenerate brain and muscle cells
- *Two or three servings of fruit and/or vegetables* to replenish the vitamins and minerals you need to avoid fatigue and help your immune system
- *One or two servings of whole grain breads or cereals* to maximize fiber, iron, and B vitamins to keep your digestion and metabolism running in high gear
- *Milk or yogurt* (three to four cups every day) or the equivalent in non-dairy sources of calcium to keep your bones strong

Mona Milius's first mission is to provide maximum variety for her students because "They expect it." From vitamin-fortified sport drinks to tofu, there are choices in her dining halls for every food preference. Never had hummus and pita bread? College is the time to venture out and try new foods. Plan to try new foods often. Ask for a bite-size serving the

Sean, who is working toward a double major in computer science and biology: *Everyone has always said breakfast is the most important meal of the day. Well, it's funny, this whole eating breakfast thing really works. I have noticed that I am more awake in class on days that I eat breakfast. Also, when I get up and eat breakfast, I am much more productive, partly because I am up earlier and have more time during the day and partly just because I am more energized.*

Aaron, who is undecided about his major and plays a lot of intramural sports: *Eating breakfast in the morning has really helped me wake up for my classes and seems to have given me more energy throughout the day.*

first time. Your mouth will be watering for stuffed portobello mush-rooms the next time they're on the menu.

Don't be shy about asking questions about ingredients in the new menu items you are trying. If the food item's label is not posted on the serving line, the food service staff at your college can check for ingredients and nutrient values.

Snacking is a good idea for weight control because it helps you avoid metabolic slowdowns. The theory is to trick your body into thinking it is constantly metabolizing food, so it never slows down. Five smaller meals a day are better than two large ones. Many colleges offer the equivalent of the University of Northern Iowa's Dining Dollars. This is a charge card or cash equivalent system that allows students to pick up snacks like a carton of milk or a bag of almonds between meals. Programs like this add flexibility to meal planning. With this type of card, students have credit at the deli or pantries around campus. It's a good idea to have the card or ready cash for bananas, apples, yogurt, orange juice, or a turkey sandwich between classes.

More Strategies from Science

The Smart Student's Guide to Healthy Living has a taste of something for everyone, and this menu of ideas comes straight from trusted nutrition scientists. If you don't want to follow the ABC list or focus on the whole and colored foods plan, there are other simple and effective ways you can reduce your total calories to control your weight.

HAVE A SALAD

Try eating a salad with reduced- fat dressing before you start your meal. Doing so allows you to eat fewer calories at each meal without even thinking about it. That is what a Penn State professor found in a study of forty-two people (Rolls 2004). People who had a salad before their main course tended to consume 12 percent fewer calories per meal than those who didn't start with a salad. A salad was defined as three cups of fresh greens and vegetables. Remember, the salad must be topped with a low-fat dressing. Also, portion size seemed to matter in this study. When people were offered 100 calories worth of salad in two different portions—one and a half cups and three cups—they ate less during the main course after the larger portion, suggesting that for salads, the bigger, the better.

The implication of this study is that when selecting a first course, diners should be aware that both the energy density and the portion size of the food affect the amount of energy they consume in the meal. If you order a salad and find no reduced-fat dressings available, the next best strategy is to select a clear dressing (versus a creamy one) because it takes a smaller portion to flavor a salad. The extra few calories would be worth it, in this case, because eating the salad may reduce intake during the meal to follow.

Aaron, a student whose major is undecided, tested having a salad with lunch and dinner: *As far as having a salad at every main meal, it has just started coming naturally to me. I always grab one and it just makes me feel like I am eating better.*

Chris, a music major from South Dakota: *The plan of eating a salad before lunch and dinner has really been a great way to get into a groove of eating healthier. My lunches have substantially decreased— in terms of the amount of entrée I take.*

Sean, a biology and computer science major: *The impression I got from testing this salad strategy was that you should eat a salad and then go back and get the rest of your food. This is good in theory, but impractical given the lines in the cafeteria. I do think simply getting a salad with your meal and eating it first is a good idea.*

THREE DAILY SERVINGS OF DAIRY

Some studies suggest that eating three servings of milk, cheese, or yogurt a day can help you lose more weight by burning more fat than you'd lose by cutting calories alone. In a study conducted by Michael Zemel and colleagues at the University of Tennessee (2004), people who following a reduced-calorie diet and consumed three servings of milk, cheese, or yogurt each day lost significantly more weight and body fat than those who didn't. Individuals were placed on one of three diets: one low in calcium and dairy, one with calcium supplements but low in dairy, and one with three daily servings of dairy. Each person consumed a diet that was 500 calories lower than their actual caloric needs. After twenty-four weeks, those on the high-dairy diet on average lost the greatest amount of body weight (11 percent) and body fat (14 percent).

In another study conducted at the University of Tennessee, this same researcher found that overweight people who added three servings of low-fat yogurt daily lost 22 percent more weight and 61 percent more body fat than did those who didn't eat yogurt (Zemel et al. 2004). The researcher suggested that yogurt's high calcium value stimulates fat loss while preserving protein.

Though these research results may sound promising, it is important to remember that the studies took place under tightly controlled dietary conditions. The most important thing to remember, however, is the bottom line: to lose weight you need to cut the calories you take in and boost the calories you use through exercise. At the same time, eating yogurt remains helpful for many other reasons:

- Yogurt may prevent constipation and diarrhea.
- Yogurt reduces the risk of colon cancer and reduces gastritis (an infection in the stomach that leads to ulcers).

- Calcium-rich dairy choices like yogurt help prevent the development of osteoporosis.

When You Don't Tolerate Dairy Foods

As beneficial as milk and dairy can be, there are lots of people who can't tolerate milk. One reason is lactose intolerance. If you experience gas, pain, discomfort, bloating, diarrhea, or constipation from drinking milk, you may not be producing adequate lactase. Lactase is the enzyme that breaks down lactose, the sugar in dairy products. When lactose does not break down, it causes gastrointestinal symptoms like bloating and gas. This problem can run in families. If you are like millions of people and are lactose intolerant, there are many dietary alternative to dairy products.

Some people find enzyme replacement products such as Lactaid Fast Act to be helpful. This supplement contains lactase, and you chew it with the first bite of a dairy food to break down the lactose. You can also find lactose-free milk on the dairy shelf and it may be an option in your college cafeteria. Be sure to ask one of the food servers.

Robin, a student who works out regularly and feels she eats pretty healthfully: *Drinking a glass of milk at every meal was really good for me since I usually don't drink milk at all.*

Aaron, who has not decided on his major: *The three glasses of milk a day habit is very easy to do. If I forget to have milk at lunch, I can easily drink three glasses at dinner. I have always kept myself away from soda. Milk is a healthy alternative and I feel like I am getting my calcium for the day.*

For those with a milk intolerance, soy beverages are also an option. Soy beverages are delicious and are available on many campuses. Be sure that your brand of soy milk has calcium added.

Other sources of calcium. If you just don't care for the taste of milk from dairy sources or soy, there are other ways to obtain calcium. Tuna, mackerel, and salmon are good sources, as are kale, spinach, navy beans, and almonds. Some tofu is rich in calcium (check the label). Orange juice is now also available with added calcium and vitamin D.

WHAT ABOUT WATER?

One last thing before we move on to snacks and recipes: Do you need to be reminded to drink water? Water, whether in cool blue bottles or carbonated in yellow cans, is very much in style on campus. Just remember that water is more than a fashion statement on the side of your backpack. It is also precious to your body and brain. Water composes up to 75 percent of your body weight, and it is involved in every physiological process in your body. Drinking water with meals and in between classes helps regulate your body temperature, carries nutrients and oxygen to your cells, and clears out wastes. It also cushions your joints and protects your organs and tissues.

How much do you need? The average college student needs about eight to twelve cups of water each day. A twenty-ounce bottle equals two and a half cups. So three or four refills a day is a good start. These are specific times to boost your fluid intake:

- During hot weather, your body perspires more, increasing water loss. Cool water is absorbed much more quickly than warm water. During the winter, water is just as vital. Forced-air heat can cause your skin to lose much-needed moisture through evaporation. You may not feel as hot, sweaty, or thirsty as you do in the summer, but you still lose water that needs to be replaced. Warm caffeine-free beverages are the best choice for replacing body water when you've been outside in cold weather.

- Eating a whole foods diet that is high in fiber also requires extra water to process the roughage and prevent constipation.

- After an aerobic workout, such as swimming or jogging, drink one to two cups of water for each half hour of activity. Sports drinks, fruit and vegetable juices, mineral water, soft drinks, and other beverages all count toward your fluid needs. Cold water or sports drinks are the fluid of choice during games or competitions. When competitions last longer than sixty minutes, sports drinks may be helpful. They contain simple carbohydrates, which move to your working muscles fast and may delay the onset of fatigue. But some athletes find sports drinks cause cramping, so experiment with them in small amounts. You lose small amounts of sodium and other minerals in sweat. These are normally replaced by the foods you eat, so sports beverages are only necessary

Derek, a political science major from Iowa, said, *The water here on campus does not taste all that great in the dorms and does not make me feel well. I have resorted to buying bottled water, but there are water filters that students on campus do use that make the water taste better.*

for those doing intense physical activities that last for an hour or more.

- If your dorm room water tastes bad and you find yourself avoiding it, invest in bottled water or a filter pitcher. Brita and PUR both make space-saver pitchers that fit a dorm room fridge. If you use one, your water will be filtered and always taste fresh. Pick up four or five replacement filters, as they have to be replaced after two months.

- Feeling fatigued? One of the first symptoms of dehydration is mild fatigue. Students who exercise, live, or work in hot environments or who are juggling a hectic schedule are at especially high risk for mild dehydration. This dehydration-fatigue connection can also create a feeling like hunger.

- To drink more water, fill a pitcher with a daily allotment and keep it on your desk, or take eight gulps of water when passing a water fountain (1 gulp equals about an ounce).

smart snacks & more than forty recipes you can prepare in the dorm

You've been introduced to two food plans for weight control and many meal planning tips. Now it's time to cook!

Snacking, a Smart Strategy

Snacks are often thought of something extra that we feel guilty about eating. This notion doesn't fit with the science. Nutritionists now agree that five or six small meals or snacks daily are healthier than one or two large ones. A snack can give you real nutrition and an energy boost, and it doesn't have to be fattening. If you enjoy a nibble between meals but are afraid that you're eating too many calories, reduce your portions at mealtime. That way you can have a snack without the guilt or extra calories. Be a smart snacker, choosing a variety of foods like those on the list below.

Fruit

- Grapes
- Bing cherries
- Strawberries
- Raspberries
- Peaches
- Citrus
- Pears
- Blueberries
- Bananas
- Dried fruit

Vegetable

- Carrots
- Cauliflower
- Celery
- Broccoli
- Tomatoes
- Vegetable soup
- Reduced-fat vegetable dip

Dairy

- Skim or 1 percent milk
- Cottage cheese
- Reduced-fat cream cheese
- Low-fat yogurt

Beverages

- 100 percent orange or other fruit juice
- V-8 or tomato juice
- Sugar-free beverages
- Mineral water
- Unsweetened teas

Grains/Nuts

- Whole wheat crackers
- Whole wheat bagels
- Whole grain cereals
- Chex Mix
- Peanuts
- Almonds
- Mixed nuts
- Trail mix
- Popcorn

Take a Calorie-Free Break

If you want to save your appetite for dinner, consider these calorie-free ways to break up a homework marathon:

- Enjoy a large glass of ice water, a cup of hot tea, or a calorie-free mineral water with a twist of lemon or lime.
- Drink a cup of mint tea.
- Brush and floss your teeth.
- Take a fifteen to thirty minute walk.
- Work on a favorite hobby.
- Keep a list of tiny but productive things you need to do, and accomplish them when you need a break from studying.

Learn to Cook

Cooking healthy meals for your friends in the dorm can be a great way to meet people, share conversation, and enjoy four-star dining. Most of this chapter is devoted to healthy recipes you can prepare in the dorm room. The recipes are divided in sections according to appliances needed. The following simple items can make cooking easy:

- Medium-sized mixing bowl
- Microwave-safe dish
- Mixing spoon
- Plastic wrap
- Measuring spoons
- Liquid measuring cup
- Flat metal baking sheet
- Can opener
- Liquid dish detergent
- Hot plate or electric heating element
- Dish scrubber
- Paper towels or dish towels

Cooking is a very individual and creative endeavor. When you look through these recipes, feel free to add other ingredients or make creative substitutions. You'll soon be known down the hall and around the corner as the one who knows how to cook! These recipes generally serve four to six hearty appetites, unless otherwise noted. When you do the shopping for your cooking, be sure to save the sales slips and divide the cost among the diners. This gives everyone a chance to contribute to the meal, which will usually cost less (and taste better) than dining out.

FOOD SAFETY FIRST

Before using the recipes, we have a quick primer for you on food safety. There are some simple food safety facts you need to be aware of. Getting sick from unsafe food, otherwise known as food poisoning, is caused when food is not handled properly during shopping, storage, and cooking. When refrigerated foods sit out at room temperature, microorganisms that cause food poisoning can grow. These disease-causing bugs include bacteria, viruses, parasites, and molds. All can cause illness, but bacteria are the most common. Here are the symptoms most often associated with food poisoning:

- diarrhea
- abdominal cramps
- vomiting
- headache
- fatigue
- mild fever
- chills
- muscle pain

These signs are similar to those of the flu. Symptoms can appear anywhere from a half hour to a week after eating a contaminated food, although four to forty-eight hours is more common. Resting and drinking plenty of fluids is the best way to treat the illness, which usually lasts a day or two. Severe symptoms, which require medical help, include bloody diarrhea, excessive vomiting, stiff neck, severe headache, blurred vision, dizziness, and high or ongoing fever. Food poisoning can be particularly dangerous and even fatal for people with weak immune systems. Thankfully, it can easily be prevented by properly storing, preparing, and cooking foods.

The Biology of Food Poisoning

To multiply, bacteria need the right set of conditions: time, a wet environment, and temperatures between 40 and 140 degrees Fahrenheit. Most bacteria thrive in protein foods like meat, poultry, fish, eggs, and dairy produces. Be very careful about purchasing and storing these items.

Safe Food Shopping & Storage

The following tips will help you ensure food safety at every step— from shopping to storing leftovers:

- Buy frozen and refrigerated foods and hot items from the deli at the end of the shopping trip. Make sure frozen foods feel solid and refrigerated foods feel cold. Get these foods back to your room fast and put them in the fridge and freezer first. If you are walking or biking home from the store, consider buying an insulated grocery bag for transport.
- Look at the sell date on refrigerated products like milk and yogurt. The *sell date* is how long the grocers can keep the product for sale on the shelf. The *use date* indicates how long you can keep the product before it begins to spoil.

- Don't buy meat, fish, or chicken that has torn packaging. When you buy fresh or frozen meat, put it in a double plastic bag at the bottom of your cart.
- Don't use cracked eggs.
- Choose cans that are free of dents, bulges, and leaks.
- Once you're back at the dorm, avoid overloading the fridge, as it's important for the cold air to circulate. Clean up spills in the fridge as soon as possible, especially juice from a package of meat.
- If you have leftovers, keep them within sight in the fridge and use them within two or three days. Discard foods if you have forgotten how old they are.
- Freeze foods in plastic airtight freezer containers, foil, moisture-proof paper, plastic bags, and other wraps that retain quality.
- For an inexpensive disinfectant, use a bleach solution with 1 part bleach to 10 parts water. Keep your microwave, blender, and countertop grill clean by washing immediately after use.
- To thaw frozen meat, place it in the refrigerator, or transfer it to a microwave-safe container and defrost on the thaw setting. Once thawed, meat or poultry must go back in the fridge or be cooked immediately. Use a clean platter or plate to serve cooked meat. Marinating meats should be placed in a covered nonmetallic container in the refrigerator.
- After a meal, divide leftovers into smaller portions and place them in shallow containers to speed cooling.

The Three Cs of Food Safety

In essence, all of the tips above boil down to three simple concepts: clean it, cook it, and cool it.

Clean it. Keep everything that comes in contact with food clean. Before cooking in your dorm room, clean and wipe off your desk or dresser top or whatever counter space you are using with a spray cleaner or soap and hot water. Consider those disposable disinfectant wipes if you don't have a sink with hot water in your room. Wash your hands with soap before you start. Use clean paper towels, sponges, dishes, and utensils. Rinse fresh foods thoroughly with cool, running water before cutting or peeling.

Cook it. Cook food thoroughly for the best insurance against food poisoning. Cooking food to an internal temperature above 160 degrees Fahrenheir kills most bacteria. If you don't have a meat or food thermometer, the best way to check meat for doneness is to be sure the juices are clear, not tinged with pink.

Cool it. Cooked food needs to be cooled rapidly so dangerous bacteria don't multiply. All cooked foods that are to be served cold should be immediately refrigerated. Chilling foods in a shallow container helps speed cooling. Don't cool food on a counter. You cannot smell or taste bacteria, so if you suspect a food has not been handled safely, don't taste it. Just throw it away.

Dorm room recipes follow. They are divided into sections based on your appliance inventory. Not every campus allows portable grilling machines. Review the recipe first for necessary cooking equipment so you can quickly decide what bowls and containers you need to borrow from next door. (Be sure to wash borrowed equipment thoroughly first, and then share leftovers with your neighbors.)

Recipes You Can Prepare in the Dorm

A word about sugar-free ingredients: Some of the following recipes suggest the use of sugar-free ingredients such as Splenda sugar substitute. These sugar-free ingredients are considered highly processed and contribute no important nutrients to the diet. However, they may be appropriate if you have a primary interest in controlling calories and carbohydrates.

NO SPECIAL APPLIANCE NEEDED

You will need a source of hot water for the beverages. First, a word about safety: Always make sure electric power cords are kept at a safe distance from water. Also, always be sure to unplug electric heating element cords from sockets when you are finished.

Sugar-Free Hot Cocoa Mix

When the dorm room feels cold, mix up some calcium-fortified hot cocoa. Use the very hottest tap water, boil water in a hot pot, or heat water in a glass measuring cup in the microwave. This recipe will make 48 servings.

- **1 8-quart box of nonfat dry milk**
- **1 1-pound box of cocoa powder**
- **1 6-ounce jar powdered coffee creamer (flavored is fine)**
- **¾ cup Splenda sugar substitute (or use ¾ cup regular sugar)**

Mix all of the ingredients together and store in a covered container. To make 1 cup of hot chocolate, stir 3 heaping tablespoons of the mix into 6 ounces (or ¾ cup) of very hot or boiling water. Stir briskly.

Spiced Tea Mix

Tea is infused with antioxidants. This is a sweet and spicy version of the drink. Use the very hottest tap water, boil water in a hot pot, or heat water in a glass measuring cup in the microwave. This recipe will make 48 servings. To prepare 2 quarts:

1 small package of sugar-free lemonade mix (such as Crystal Light)

2 cups sugar-free Tang

1 cup Splenda sugar substitute

1 cup instant tea powder (such as unflavored Nestea)

2 tablespoons ground cinnamon

Mix all of the ingredients together in a covered container. To make a cup of tea, stir 2 heaping tablespoons of the mix into 6 ounces (or ¾ cup) hot water.

Gorp

You can take baggies of this savory, sweet snack, which is full of fiber, to the library. This recipe will make 32 servings.

1 10-ounce can salted peanuts or mixed nuts

1 15-ounce box raisins

1 7-ounce jar sunflower kernels

1 6-ounce package dried cranberries (also sold as Craisins)

Mix everything together and store in a covered container. Dispense into baggies as needed.

43

RECIPES USING REFRIGERATED INGREDIENTS

Salsa Ranch Dip

It's Friday afternoon. Whip up a party!

Serves 8-12

1 1-ounce package ranch-style dressing mix

2 8-ounce cups light sour cream

$^2/_3$ cup thick and chunky salsa

In a small mixing bowl, mix all of the ingredients together and chill for at least 30 minutes. Serve with yellow corn chips.

Fresh Fruit Dip

This dip keeps well for a week, refrigerated.

1 8-ounce tub strawberry-flavored cream cheese, softened

1 8-ounce container sugar-free strawberry yogurt

2 cups nonfat whipped topping

Fresh fruits for dipping, such as sliced apples, pears, or bananas or whole strawberries or grapes

In a medium mixing bowl, mix the cream cheese, yogurt, and whipped topping together, cover with plastic wrap, and chill. Serve with the fruit.

Creamy Feta and Herb Spread

Feta cheese has a robust flavor but is not as intense as blue cheese. Try it!

1 package feta cheese, crumbled

1 8-ounce package light cream cheese, softened

1 tablespoon dried basil

½ cup chopped pecans

Mix all of the ingredients together in a small bowl, cover tightly, and chill. Spread on whole wheat bread, toast, or wheat crackers. This spread keeps for two weeks, refrigerated.

Guacamole

It's that green dip required for an authentic Mexican fiesta!

1 soft ripe avocado

½ cup salsa

1 8-ounce cup light sour cream

Peel the avocado using a sharp knife, then pare the flesh off the stone. Mash flesh with a fork on a plate or flat surface. In a small bowl, combine the mashed avocado with the salsa and sour cream. Serve with corn chips.

Grilled Chicken Salad

Look for bright colors and crisp greens when buying bagged salad mixes. You can find grilled chicken strips in the processed meat section of the store.

1 10-ounce bag mixed greens

1 8-ounce package grilled chicken strips

1 8-ounce package shredded Monterey Jack and Cheddar cheese

2 tablespoons of your favorite salad dressing

Portion the lettuce onto 4 plates. Top with the grilled chicken, cheese, and dressing.

Crunchy Chicken Salad

This is tasty on 100 percent whole wheat bread. Serve with a dill pickle on the side.

1 12-ounce can white meat chicken, drained

½ cup chopped nuts

1 green onion, chopped

2 stalks celery, chopped

²/₃ cup light mayonnaise

Combine all of the ingredients together in a medium mixing bowl. Serve immediately or chill.

Tuna Salad

Look for the words "light tuna" on product labels. This is generally preferred due to mercury levels in some fattier brands.

1 14-ounce can or pouch light tuna, drained

1 green onion, diced fine

1 stalk celery, diced fine

½ cup light mayonnaise

Combine all of the ingredients together in a medium mixing bowl. Serve immediately or chill.

Seven-Layer Salad

Remember this from family reunions? If you don't want to mix your own dressing, then substitute light ranch, light blue cheese, or light creamy italian from the bottle.

- **1 10-ounce bag lettuce**
- **2 ribs celery, diced fine**
- **1 small red onion, diced fine**
- **1 10-ounce box frozen peas, thawed and drained well**
- **1 cup light mayonnaise**
- **2 tablespoons Splenda sugar substitute or regular sugar**
- **2 tablespoons vinegar or lemon juice**
- **12 ounces shredded Cheddar cheese**
- **¼ cup real bacon bits (such as Oscar Mayer Real Bacon in a pouch)**

In a 9 by 13-inch cake pan or disposable metal tray, layer the lettuce, diced onion, celery, and peas. In a small bowl, combine the mayonnaise, sugar substitute, and vinegar. Spread over the peas. Top with the cheese and bacon. Cover and refrigerate for at least 1 hour. Best eaten within 24 hours.

Tabbouleh

- **1 5-ounce box cracked wheat (such as Near East brand)**
- **1 cucumber, peeled and diced**
- **1 tomato, diced**
- **½ cup reduced-fat Italian dressing**
- **1 cup shredded Parmesan cheese**

Boil water and prepare the cracked wheat in a heat-safe salad bowl according to the package directions. Cool to room temperature. Combine with the remaining ingredients, cover, and chill.

Crab Spread

Spread this on a whole grain bagel when you need a quick lunch. For shrimp lovers, substitute a can of shrimp. Chop them well before adding to the spread. Cocktail sauce is red and is sold near the ketchup and meat sauces.

1 8-ounce package light cream cheese, softened

$\frac{1}{4}$ cup milk

$\frac{1}{3}$ cup cocktail sauce

$\frac{1}{2}$ to 1 cup diced celery

1 5-ounce can flaked crab, drained well

Combine all of the ingredients together in a small mixing bowl. Cover with plastic wrap and chill. Serve with whole grain crackers or chips.

Popeye's Favorite Dip

No kidding about the nutritional punch in this recipe—spinach is a potent source of vitamin A and iron!

1 10-ounce box frozen spinach, thawed and squeezed free of liquid

2 8-ounce cups light sour cream

1 envelope Knorr vegetable soup mix

Mix all of the ingredients together in a medium mixing bowl. Cover with plastic wrap and chill for at least 1 hour. Serve with whole grain crackers.

Layered Taco Dip

Get out the paper plates and napkins for this one!

 1 8-ounce package light cream cheese, softened

 2 8-ounce cups light sour cream

 1 1-ounce envelope taco seasoning mix

 1 1-pound bag shredded lettuce

 1 cup shredded Cheddar cheese

 1 green onion, diced

 1 green pepper, diced

 Corn chips, for dipping

In a small mixing bowl, combine the cream cheese, sour cream, and taco seasoning. Use a knife or spatula to spread this out over a large round platter. Layer the lettuce on top, then sprinkle with the cheese, then the onion and green pepper. Serve with corn chips. Use a spoon to serve onto paper plates, or everyone huddle around the tray and start dipping.

Burrito Bites

Great for Sunday night suppers!

 1 8-ounce package light cream cheese

 1 8-ounce carton light sour cream

 1 4-ounce can green chiles, chopped

 1 4-ounce can black olives, chopped

 1 green onion, chopped

 1 green pepper, chopped

 1 cup shredded Cheddar cheese

 1 8-ounce package small, whole grain, soft tortillas

In a medium mixing bowl, combine the cream cheese, sour cream, green chiles, olives, green onion, green pepper, and cheese. Spread onto the tortillas, roll up, and cut into bite-size pieces. These may be stored in a covered container in the refrigerator for up to 3 days. But they won't last that long!

Cucumber Sandwiches

These are always a hit! Leave the peel on the cucumber to add color and fiber.

1 teaspoon seasoned salt

1 8-ounce package light cream cheese, softened

24 slices cocktail rye bread

2 large cucumbers, sliced into 24 slices

1 tablespoon dried dill weed

In a small mixing bowl, stir the seasoned salt into the cream cheese. Spread onto one side of each slice of bread, and top each with cucumber slice. Sprinkle with the dill. Serve on a tray or platter.

Broccoli Main Dish Salad

This meal in a salad bowl lasts for three days in the fridge.

Florets from 1 large bunch of broccoli, chopped fine

1 red onion, thinly sliced

¼ pound Canadian bacon or ham, diced

½ cup raisins

1 cup reduced-fat creamy italian or ranch with bacon dressing

Combine all of the ingredients together in a salad bowl. Mix well, cover, and chill.

Fruit in Paradise

This is a sweet treat when you get back from the gym or the track.

1 8-ounce can pineapple tidbits in juice, drained

1 cup red grapes

2 kiwifruits, peeled and diced

1 8-ounce carton piña colada yogurt

Combine all of the ingredients together in a medium bowl. Cover and chill.

Frozen Fruit Cups

Delicious and satisfying! You are in charge of your sweet tooth!

2 bananas

1 10-ounce box frozen unsweetened raspberries or strawberries, thawed

1 8-ounce can pineapple tidbits

1 12-ounce can sugar-free Sprite or 7-Up

Combine all of the ingredients in a large bowl. Mix well, then portion out into clear plastic cups and freeze for at least 4 hours. To eat, allow to thaw 10 minutes at room temperature, or microwave for 45 seconds.

Banana Cream Pie

Are you parents coming for a visit? Surprise them with a pie!

3 firm ripe bananas

1 prepared shortbread crust

1 3-ounce box sugar-free instant pudding

1½ cups milk

2 cups fat-free whipped topping

Peel and slice the bananas into the shortbread crust. In a small bowl, combine the pudding and milk and stir vigorously for 3 minutes. Pour over the bananas. Top with whipped topping. Chill for at least 1 hour.

RECIPES USING A MICROWAVE

Three-Bean Cowboy Casserole

It is delicious and filling. Legume-based main dishes are a protein-rich way to experience vegetarian dining.

- **1 8-ounce can kidney beans, drained**
- **1 16-ounce can Bush's hot and spicy baked beans**
- **1 8-ounce can butter beans, drained**
- **1 small onion, chopped very fine**
- **8 ounces lean ham or Canadian bacon, chopped (optional)**

Combine all of the ingredients together in a microwave-safe bowl or dish. Cover the top of the bowl with a paper towel to avoid splattering the microwave. Microwave on high power for 5 minutes. Stir. Microwave for 3 to 5 more minutes.

Bavarian Kraut Casserole

Your dorm room is going to smell like Germany! Be sure to buy some rye bread to accompany this dish. Adding the Splenda will intensify the sweet-and-sour flavor.

- **1 16-ounce can Bavarian sauerkraut, drained**
- **8 ounces Canadian bacon, diced**
- **1 16-ounce can diced potatoes, drained**
- **1 green onion, diced**
- **¼ cup Splenda sugar substitute (optional)**

Combine all of the ingredients together in a microwave-safe bowl or dish. Cover the top with a paper towel to avoid splattering in the microwave. Microwave on high power for 5 minutes. Stir. Microwave for 3 to 5 more minutes.

Scalloped Potatoes and Ham

Feeling lonesome for home? Invite the neighbors over for a taste from grandma's kitchen.

$2^3/_4$ cups hot water

$^1/_3$ cup milk

I tablespoon butter

I 5-ounce package of Betty Crocker's Three Cheese Potatoes

8 ounces lean sliced ham

Combine the water, milk, butter, and the potatoes and their sauce in a 2-quart microwave-safe bowl. Microwave uncovered on 100% power for 10 to 15 minutes, stirring every 5 minutes. Stir the ham in at the end of cooking time. Allow to sit for 3 minutes before serving.

Ragin' Cajun Red Beans and Rice

If you can't make it to Mardi Gras, you can still enjoy the taste of New Orleans.

I 8-ounce package Zatarain's Red Beans and Rice mix

8 ounces shredded mozzarella cheese

Prepare the Zatarain's mix in a microwave-safe bowl or dish according to the package directions. Serve with the shredded cheese on the side.

Sloppy Joes

This recipe makes 8 sandwiches. Add whole grain chips, bananas, and milk to create a meal for your new dorm family. A savory and filling meal for cold days and nights.

I pound lean ground beef

I cup Manwich sauce

8 whole wheat buns

In a microwave-safe bowl, cook the ground beef on 100% power for 3 minutes. Then use a wooden spoon to break it up. Continue cooking for 3 more minutes, then stir again. Cook for 3 more minutes, at which point it should be uniformly brown. To prevent clogging, do not pour the excess juice down the sink. Instead, drain the juices away into a covered container (like an old margarine container) and discard when cool. Add the Manwich sauce and cook for 2 minutes until the mixture is bubbly. Serve on the whole wheat buns.

Spaghetti

Ask your roomie to buy the salad and bread and you'll be in your own Italian restaurant. Serves 2.

4 ounces (one half of an 8-ounce box) whole wheat spaghetti

I 8-ounce jar marinara sauce with meat (such as Ragú or Prego)

8 ounces shredded Parmesan cheese

In a large microwave-safe dish, break the spaghetti into bite-sized pieces. Cover with water 2 inches above the noodles, then cover the dish tightly with a microwave-safe top. Microwave on high power for 10 minutes. carefully, remove the cover to allow the steam to escape without burning your fingers. Taste one of the noodles for doneness. It should be tender, not hard. If it is not done, you may need to add more water. Re-cover and heat for 3 more minutes, then continue to test for doneness. Drain the noodles and stir in the marinara sauce. Heat for 2 more minutes. Serve with the Parmesan cheese on the side.

Scrambled Eggs

Fix Sunday breakfast in your room. Serves 1.

3 whole eggs

$^2/_3$ cup milk

Salt and pepper

Optional toppings: diced ham, shredded cheese, salsa

In a flat microwave-safe dish, whip the eggs and milk together with a fork until smooth. Sprinkle with salt and pepper to taste. Microwave on high power for 3 minutes. Stir to break up the eggs, then cook for 1 or 2 more minutes. Serve with whatever toppings you prefer.

Nachos

Black beans make these a meal.

1 12-ounce bag corn chips

1 16-ounce can black beans, drained well

1 4-ounce can sliced jalapeño peppers

8 ounces shredded Monterrey Jack and Cheddar cheese

¾ cup salsa

On a large microwave-safe plate, arrange the corn chips to cover the surface. Then sprinkle with the beans and peppers. Sprinkle with the cheese. Microwave for 2 minutes on 100% power, until cheese is soft and melted. Serve with the salsa on the side.

Baked Potatoes with Toppings

Eat those chewy potato skins—that's where the fiber hides.

4 large Russet baking potatoes

Toppings: Diced ham, shredded cheese, light sour cream, chopped green onions

Wash the potatoes well. Pierce them on each side eight times with a fork. Place in the microwave and cook on 100% power for 10 minutes, turning them twice during the cooking time. Serve with toppings.

Broccoli and Chicken Casserole

Broccoli is rich in fiber and indoles, plant chemicals that are known to prevent damage to cellular DNA by carcinogens.

1 10-ounce box frozen chopped broccoli, thawed and drained or squeezed free of water

1 14-ounce can reduced-fat cream of chicken soup

1 10-ounce can white meat chicken, drained

1 16-ounce package Uncle Ben's Chicken Flavored Rice Mix

1½ cups water

Combine all of the ingredients together in a large microwave-safe bowl or dish. Cover the top of the dish with a paper towel to avoid splattering the microwave. Microwave on high power for 5 minutes. Stir. Microwave for 3 to 5 more minutes. Stir and taste to be sure the rice is tender and cooked through.

Meatless Chili

The all-American comfort food.

1 12-ounce jar chunky salsa

2 12-ounce cans chili-flavored tomatoes

2 16-ounce cans chili-flavored kidney beans

Toppings: shredded cheese, light sour cream, chopped green onions

Combine the salsa, tomatoes, and kidney beans in a large microwave-safe bowl. Cover with a paper towel. Microwave on 100% power for 3 minutes. Stir. Microwave for 3 to 5 more minutes. Serve in bowls with toppings and whole grain crackers.

Hot Parmesan and Artichoke Dip

This is a Mediterranean favorite, sure to add sophistication to your next party.

1 14-ounce can artichoke hearts, drained and chopped fine

1 cup grated Parmesan cheese

½ cup light mayonnaise

½ cup light sour cream

1 teaspoon black pepper

Mix all of the ingredients together in a microwave-safe bowl or dish. Cover with a paper towel. Microwave on 100% power for 3 minutes. Stir. Microwave for 3 more minutes. Serve with whole grain crackers.

Fiery Bean Dip

1 16-ounce can refried beans

4 ounces Cheddar cheese, shredded

1 cup chunky salsa

Combine all of the ingredients in a medium microwave-safe bowl or dish. Cover the top with a paper towel. Microwave on 100% power for 3 minutes. Stir. Microwave 3 to 5 more minutes until the dip is smooth and bubbly. Serve with yellow corn chips.

RECIPES USING A PORTABLE GRILLING MACHINE

If your college allows grilling machines, like those marketed by George Foreman, you can prepare flavorful lean meats a few days per week or for the Saturday tailgate party. A note of caution: Follow directions for use of the grilling machine. Be careful not to touch the hot surface of the grill, and use the handles or knobs and oven mitts to manipulate the cover. After using the grill, use the plastic scraper that comes with it to quickly remove food residue before it dries on. Always be sure the unit is turned off when you are finished. As for portion sizes, when purchasing protein foods, allow four to six ounces of meat per serving. Use these recipes to add deep flavor to plain meats.

Grilled Steaks

1 pound sirloin steak, cut into 4 pieces

¼ cup teriyaki sauce

Marinate the steak with the sauce in a large resealable bag for at least 30 minutes in the refrigerator. Then grill according to the grill's directions on medium to high heat for 8 to 10 minutes or until fully done. To test for doneness, slice into thickest part of steak. Medium steak is pink in the middle.

Grilled Salmon

1 pound salmon steak, cut into 4 pieces

2 tablespoons lemon juice

Marinate the salmon with the lemon juice in a large resealable bag for at least 30 minutes in the refrigerator or up to 4 hours. Then grill on medium to high heat for 3 to 6 minutes or until fully done. To test for doneness, salmon should flake apart when pierced with a fork.

Grilled Chicken Breast

1 pound skinless boneless chicken breast

$\frac{1}{3}$ cup Italian dressing

Marinate the chicken with the dressing in a large resealable bag for at least 30 minutes in the refrigerator. Then grill on medium to high heat for 8 to 10 minutes or until fully done. To test for doneness, slice into the center of chicken breast; it should be uniformly white.

Hamburgers

$\frac{1}{2}$ teaspoon minced garlic

1 pound lean ground beef

Mix the garlic into the beef and form into 4 patties. Grill on medium to high heat for 7 to 9 minutes or until fully cooked. Well-done hamburger has a uniform brown color through the meat.

Grilled Pork Chops

4 4-ounce boneless pork chops

$\frac{1}{4}$ cup soy sauce

Marinate the chops with the sauce in a large resealable bag at for least 30 minutes in the refrigerator. Then grill on medium to high heat for 6 to 9 minutes or until fully cooked. To test for doneness, slice into the thickest part of the chop; it should be uniformly white.

RECIPES USING A BLENDER

Here's a tip about cleaning the blender to avoid the buildup of food gunk. After pouring the food out of the blender, fill the blender container with water and hit "pulse." This will briskly rinse the container and make cleanup much easier.

Hummus

This is a delicious high-protein snack from Greece.

- 1 15-ounce can garbanzo beans
- ¾ cup tahini (sesame seed paste)
- 2 teaspoons lemon juice
- ½ teaspoon salt
- ½ teaspoon pepper
- 2 teaspoons parsley or basil

In a blender, combine the garbanzo beans, tahini, and lemon juice and blend until smooth. Pour into a bowl. Stir in the salt, pepper, and parsley or basil. Serve with whole grain pita bread.

Orange Jubilee

This makes two 12-ounce servings. Leftover Orange Jubilee can be frozen.

- 1 6-ounce can frozen orange juice concentrate
- 1 cup milk
- ½ cup Splenda sugar substitute
- 2 cups small ice cubes

Blend all of the ingredients until smooth. Serve immediately.

Strawberry Banana Smoothie

All of these smoothie recipes can be modified according to your taste. Substitute peach for pineapple or orange for lemon. Make it up as you go along. Yogurt is a calcium-rich winner in any combo.

1 firm ripe banana

1 8-ounce carton sugar-free strawberry yogurt

Blend until smooth.

Pineapple Lemon Smoothie

1 8-ounce carton sugar-free lemon yogurt

½ cup pineapple tidbits

Blend until smooth.

Coffee Smoothie

1 8-ounce carton sugar-free vanilla yogurt

½ cup cold strong coffee

Blend until smooth.

Best Choices When Eating Off Campus

For a quick meal on the run, a change of pace, or a special evening of elegant dining, eating off campus will be a memorable part of your college lifestyle. With a little planning, eating out can be a healthy choice and fit into your dorm room diet. Some of the problems with restaurant meals, however, include high levels of calories, fat, and sodium, too little fiber, and scant vitamins and minerals.

Don't be shy. If you don't understand a menu description, ask the waiter or counter attendant, "Can you please tell me how this is prepared?" Be specific in asking to hold the butter or requesting dressing on the side. It might be best to pass up the buffet and unlimited salad bars. Remember, stop eating before you feel completely full. Ask to take the food left on your plate back to your dorm room and then refrigerate it immediately.

SANDWICH SHOP OR THE DELI

- Whole grain breads with meat, cheese, lettuce, tomatoes, onions, peppers, cucumbers, fresh herbs, or sprouts.
- Consider eating just half the bread.
- Ask for light cheese and light mayonnaise. Or, ask for a small green salad on the side, with low-fat dressing, instead of chips.
- The best salad dressings are fat-free italian or red wine vinaigrette.

PIZZA

- Ask for a whole grain crust, or choose the thinnest crust.
- Add Canadian bacon or chicken for lean protein, plus onion, pepper, mushroom, pineapple, or sauerkraut.
- Always have a green salad with lots of fresh veggies and reduced-fat dressing.

CHINESE

- Stir-fried plain meat and vegetable combinations (rather than breaded, deep-fried meats) such as
  - Beef and chicken with Chinese vegetables
  - Snow white chicken
  - Pork with vegetables
  - Shrimp with vegetables
- Vegetarian entrees
- Vegetable chow mein
- Wonton soup
- Hot-and-sour soup
- Ask if whole grain brown rice is available. Full of nutrients and fiber, it's better for you than white rice.

THAI FOOD

- Chicken soup with coconut milk
- Hot shrimp soup
- Fried mixed vegetables
- Hot cabbage salad
- Omelet with vegetables and minced pork
- Steamed rice
- Hot curry with chicken or shrimp
- Pumpkin in coconut milk
- Plantain in coconut milk

FAMILY RESTAURANT

- Soups with vegetables
- Broccoli-Cheddar soup
- French onion soup
- Chili
- Fresh vegetable plate
- Steamed vegetables
- Garden, spinach, Greek, or cucumber salad
- Chef salad
- Seafood salad
- Grilled chicken salad
- Coleslaw
- Three-bean salad
- Steak or chops
- Broiled or grilled chicken or fish
- Baked potato in the skin
- Brown rice
- Burger or grilled chicken on a whole-grain bun

MEXICAN

- Black bean soup
- Salsa topping (versus sour cream or guacamole)
- Taco salad
- Bean, beef, pork, or chicken yellow corn tostada, burrito, quesadilla, or taco (using a yellow corn tortilla, not a fried shell)
- Refried beans

ITALIAN

- Minestrone soup
- Green salad with clear dressing
- Whole grain breadsticks
- Whole grain or spinach pasta with vegetables, chicken, seafood, or lean beef toppings in a red sauce or broth-based sauce (not a buttery, rich Alfredo-type sauce)
- Cappuccino

FAST-FOOD BURGER

The supersize deals are a fast ticket to weight gain, so avoid them unless you're going to share the order with a friend.

- Whole grain buns
- Broiled or charbroiled single or quarter-pound burger with lettuce, tomato, and onion
- Grilled chicken
- Baked potato with broccoli or chili topping
- Green salad with grilled chicken or shrimp

BREAKFAST OUT

- Whole grain waffles with fruit topping
- Whole wheat French toast with fruit topping
- Whole grain cereal with 1 percent or skim milk
- Sugar-free yogurt with fresh fruit
- Omelet or scrambled egg with lean ham, cheese, and lots of vegetables

- Breakfast ham or lean pork sausage
- Whole wheat toast or English muffins
- Wheat or bran muffins with raisins or nuts

DESSERT

- Fruit ice and sorbet
- Low-fat frozen yogurt or ice cream
- Fresh fruit
- Angel food cake
- Cappuccino

BEVERAGES

Always add milk or 100 percent orange or other fruit juice to your meals off campus, or choose the following:

- Sugar-free soft drinks
- Mineral water
- Unsweetened teas or coffee
- Crystal Light or sugar-free flavored drinks

Staying Motivated

The trouble with any kind of diet change is that it's much easier to start a new program than it is to keep it going. Beginning to eat whole foods or foods from the A list is easier than continuing the practice over the long haul. With this diet plan, expect that you will have to continue to motivate yourself. You may become bored or restless when the results of diet change come too slowly.

SEVEN WAYS TO KICK-START OR SUSTAIN HEALTHY CHOICES

Use these tips to continually fine-tune your new habits.

1. Keep trying something new. Never had a raspberry smoothie? Go ahead and try it the next time you're in the café on campus, even if has not appealed to you before. You may actually like it! Never sipped a black bean soup? Now may be the time to try what many vegetarians consider the next thing to heaven.

2. Keep mixing things up. To prevent boredom with foods on the A list, don't eat the same combination of foods day in and day out. Vary your menu. Most Americans eat the same fifteen to twenty foods each week. Choose to be creative with your mealtime decisions.

3. Find time. You can choose to sabotage your plan to avoid the freshman fifteen by employing a whole host of excuses. "I don't have time to eat right" is the most common one. If making it to the cafeteria for a healthy breakfast seems like too much of a challenge after waking up and getting dressed, then down a bottle of orange juice and call it good. But then schedule time for a yogurt in the midmorning.

4. Be flexible. Things happen. You oversleep. A treasured relationship is in trouble. You miss your afternoon workout because of a meeting that went on too long. You travel out of town over the weekend and can't find any foods on the A list. You get sick and your work piles up. Unexpected events, illnesses, and schedule snafus are part of life. Don't let them permanently distract you from your goal. Readjust. Refocus. But keep moving forward.

5. Find support. Making a food behavior change is hard work, especially on your own. You will be much more successful if you find others who are making the same kinds of changes. Send a daily email home to your parents to keep them updated on your progress. Work on it with a friend. Working on healthy eating with someone can give you more motivation.

6. Internal rewards. After each A list choice at the cafeteria, reflect on those choices and what you have accomplished. Ask yourself, "Do I feel satisfied, in control, and energized?" Developing these kinds of internal messages and rewards will help you make a long-term commitment to healthy eating. External rewards are also a good tool, if used occasionally. Treat yourself to a manicure or a new movie release after meeting a personal goal.

7. Have fun. Avoiding the freshman fifteen should not be hard work. If it is, then something may be wrong with the process. Don't blame yourself before double-checking the process. If you are feeling hungry, are you selecting a fruit and low-fat milk at each meal? Did you select whole and colored foods for your last meal? A negative feeling or low energy could signal a lack of nutrient-rich foods from the A list. *The Smart Student's Guide to Healthy Living* can help you get back on track and feeling good again.

the freshman fifteen, food allergies & fighting fatigue: answers to the most common nutrition questions

In this chapter, you will hear from college freshmen who got the flu, misused caffeine, and found themselves without enough energy. This chapter will answer common questions about topics such as low-carbohydrate diets, alcohol, and even marijuana.

Diet Treatment for Fatigue

Meet Lisa, a vocal performance major. She was staying up late for ear training and music theory classes, and said, "I just don't have the energy I need after a long day of classes. I lack get-up-and-go."

The most common cause of fatigue among college students and young adults is inadequate sleep (read all about it in chapter 5). But if you have ruled out sleep loss as a cause of fatigue, there are smart food selection strategies you can use to boost your energy level.

First, it's important to talk about water, because the first symptom of dehydration is fatigue. The vast majority of healthy people adequately meet their daily fluid needs by drinking whenever they are thirsty. For healthy women, meeting fluid needs can mean consuming up to an average of eleven cups of water each day. For healthy men, it can mean consuming about sixteen cups. These fluid levels meet the needs of average adults but may not meet the needs of people who are very physically active, such as those who walk two hours a day between classes or those who live in hot climates.

About three-quarters of total water intake comes from drinking water and beverages. Water in food actually provides the other one-quarter of needed fluid intake. Water in food comes mostly from fruits and vegetables. Watermelon, cantaloupe, oranges, apples, and big green salads are foods that help meet our fluid needs.

A smart strategy is to drink water between meals whenever you think about thirst and preferably before your mouth feels dry. Yes, carrying a water bottle to class in the morning and refilling it after lunch is not just trendy, it's also a good idea.

Next, let's focus on simple sugars. They too can be a cause of fatigue. Simple sugars from candy bars, soft drinks, and cookies travel rapidly into the bloodstream and give us a quick energy boost. But then we bottom out. Why? Insulin production rises rapidly to clear the rush of sugar from your bloodstream. This can leave you either sleepy or jittery. Young adults need to avoid quick sugar fixes and choose whole and colored foods and A list foods.

Your diet prescription to prevent fatigue is to get plenty of fluids, reduce intake of simple sugars, and maximize intake of lean proteins, low-fat dairy foods, whole fruits and vegetables, and whole grains. These selections provide the most nutrition per calorie and will ensure your vitamin, mineral, protein, fiber, and micronutrient needs are met at the cellular level. If your cells are hydrated, well-fed from a nutrient-rich diet, and not sluggish from an infusion of sugar, you will feel energized.

Foods to Boost Mental Performance

Jane is a freshman who hasn't declared a major. In fact, she is thinking about transferring. She struggled with classes, and when interviewed at the end of her freshman year, she said, "Looking back, I realize how unhealthy I ate. I guess I just didn't realize it. It takes an effort to eat healthy."

So, knowing that academic success is the bottom line in the college experience, what food strategies can you use to boost your mental performance? The point is, while there will be times when you will feel like falling asleep in the library after lunch, it usually happens when you load up on pasta and French bread and skip the chicken breast. Metabolizing carbohydrates produces body chemicals that help us relax and can even induce sleep. A midday meal needs to include a healthy portion of lean protein, like lean roast beef or black beans. Working together, carbohydrate metabolism is slowed by the protein, and this nutrient combination is likely to produce a longer feeling of alertness. Optimal mental concentration is enhanced by an adequate intake of vitamins and minerals, so choose a midafternoon snack of fresh fruit or skim milk to keep going until your to-do list is done.

Protein adds another benefit. Protein can jump-start your brain's production of dopamine and norepinephrine, two chemicals that also keep you focused and alert.

Here's a list of lean proteins to choose from at midday. Remember to choose some carbohydrate as well. These energy nutrients work together for optimal mental performance.

- Lean ham, roast beef, or turkey
- Farmers, mozzarella, or string cheese
- Boiled egg
- Grilled chicken or pork fillet
- Grilled turkey breast
- Roast beef or roast pork
- Grilled tuna, halibut, cod, or whitefish
- Grilled salmon
- Shrimp
- Tofu
- Almonds
- Peanut butter
- Dried beans

Risks & Benefits of Caffeine

Alan is a lot like other college freshmen. He described trying to finish a research paper, saying, "I ate chocolate candy bars and drank colas to keep going late at night."

Caffeine from soda and candy, in moderation, is generally safe. Moderation means one to four servings a day. You should limit your caffeine intake to no more than 100 mg per day. That would be three cans of cola. However, caffeine is hidden in many sodas, juice drinks, and snacks, and you may simply be unaware of it.

Signs of caffeine overdose include cramps, diarrhea, jitteriness, and nausea. If you are dependent on a morning high from a supersized Mountain Dew, don't quit cold turkey. Headaches may result. Gradually reduce your intake of caffeine to a safe level.

Check out this analysis, as reported by *Consumer Reports* (2003):

Soft drink	mg caffeine per 8-ounce serving
Sunkist Orange Soda	23
Red Fusion	38
Mountain Dew	37
Pepsi	27
Pepsi Blue Berry Cola Fusion	26
Coca-Cola Classic	24
Vanilla Coke	21
Barq's Olde Tyme Root Beer	15

The following soft drinks are caffeine free: Minute Maid Orange, Slice, Sprite, 7-Up, Mug Root Beer, and caffeine-free versions of Mountain Dew.

Fruit and blended drinks	mg caffeine per 8-ounce serving
Glacéau Vitaminwater	21
Starbucks Coffee Frappuccino	83
Red Bull Energy Drink	70
Snapple Lemon Iced Tea	19
Nestea Lemon Sweetened Tea	10
Carnation Chocolate Hot Cocoa Mix	2

The following drinks are caffeine free: herbal iced tea, lemonade, fruit juice, milk, tap water, or plain bottled water.

Snacks	mg caffeine per serving
Dannon low-fat coffee yogurt, 6-ounces	36
Starbucks Java Chip ice cream, ½ cup	28
Häagen-Dazs coffee ice cream, ½ cup	24
M&M's milk chocolate candies, ¼ cup	8
Hershey's Kisses, milk chocolate, 9 pieces	5
Hershey's choclate syrup, 2 tbsp.	5
Breyers chocolate ice cream, ½ cup	3

Bottom Line on Vitamins & Minerals

Maybe you took those Flintstone chewables as a kid. But now that you're in college and Mom and Dad aren't doing the cooking, vitamin and mineral nutrition is a serious matter. Collectively known as *micro-nutrients*, vitamins are needed in the body to perform chemical reactions. The need for these nutrients varies with age, gender, level of activity, and whether or not you are pregnant. The dietary reference intakes (DRIs) are used on food labels. These numbers tell you what percent of your daily nutrient need is met by a defined portion of a food. For example, one cup of orange juice meets 120 percent of your daily need for vitamin C.

In case you forgot your junior high science class, vitamins fit into two categories: fat-soluble and water-soluble. Fat-soluble vitamins include A, D, E, and K. They are transported through the bloodstream by fat and are easily stored in the fatty tissues of the body. Water-soluble vitamins circulate through the blood. Excesses are filtered out by the kidneys and then removed in urine. Because of this, water-soluble vitamins are not easily stored and usually need replacement daily. If your college cafeteria serves liver, take a slice. It is a rich source of fat- and water-soluble vitamins because animals store nutrients in that organ. Here's the lowdown on essential vitamins and minerals.

Vitamin A. Fat-soluble, vitamin A is derived from beta-carotene, a powerful antioxidant. It is also an ingredient in some treatments for acne. Vitamin A is found in eggs, liver, fortified milk, sweet potatoes, carrots, mango, spinach, red bell pepper, apricots, and cantaloupe.

Vitamin B_1. Also known as thiamin, this vitamin works in the nervous system and in energy production. It is thought to be made inactive by the ingredients in coffee. Thiamin is present in whole grain bread, rice, pasta, and cereal.

Other B vitamins. While riboflavin (B_2), niacin (B_3), and pyridoxine (B_6) are present in fresh fruits, vegetables, and whole grains, they are also plentiful in eggs, poultry, fish, meat, and legumes, like peanuts and beans. Some vegetarians and vegans may have difficulty in obtaining vitamin B_{12}, however. This is because vitamin B_{12}, unlike other vitamins and minerals, is only found in foods of animal origin.

Biotin. Biotin helps our cellular enzymes act on amino acids. It is present in eggs, wheat germ, and oatmeal.

Vitamin C. You have probably heard that vitamin C may help prevent colds. However, it also helps maintain the strength of blood vessels, bones, and teeth. Vitamin C is found in all citrus fruits, like oranges, grapefruits, and tangerines. Berries, melons, peppers, potatoes, and tomatoes are also rich sources.

Vitamin D. This vitamin is particularly unusual because it can be made by our skin cells when we are exposed to sunlight. We actually recommend moderate exposure to the sun, with sunscreen, for this reason. Since daytime sunlight is reduced during winter, when days are shorter, you also have to drink milk and eat dairy products, eggs, tuna, or liver to get enough vitamin D. This nutrient regulates calcium and phosphorus absorption.

Vitamin E. Vitamin E's best benefit is that it protects your body's cell membranes. It can be found in safflower oil and in spreads and salad dressings that contain safflower oil, as well as in nuts, seeds, wheat germ, and green leafy vegetables.

Folic acid. Otherwise known as folate, folic acid is responsible for protein and red blood cell formation. It is the most commonly deficient vitamin in the world and is destroyed easily by heat and light. Folate deficiencies in pregnant women have been linked to birth defects. Folic acid is found in fruits, green leafy vegetables, and grains.

Vitamin K. This vitamin aids blood clotting and also helps in the maintenance of bone health. Vitamin K is produced in the body from bacteria in the intestines. Food sources include spinach, broccoli, and eggs.

Calcium. This mineral is what bones are made of. Remember your aunt with the humpback? Osteoporosis is the endgame in a calcium-deficient diet. Calcium is found in milk, yogurt, cheese, kale, broccoli, bok choy, tuna and salmon with bones, calcium-fortified soy milk, and some tofu.

Phosphorus. Phosphorus helps build strong bones and teeth. This mineral is in milk, perch, lean beef, cheese, kidney beans, and tofu.

Magnesium. Like calcium, magnesium is also involved in maintaining bones and teeth. Magnesium works to regulate body temperature. It can be found in spinach, peanut butter, pecans, and whole wheat.

Chromium. This is a micronutrient that works with insulin to help your body use glucose and maintain normal blood sugar levels. It is present in meat, eggs, whole grains, and cheese.

Copper. Copper works with zinc to keep cells defended from carcinogens. Copper is found in liver, seafood, nuts, and seeds.

Fluoride. Fluoride is famous for fighting tooth decay. It is not found widely in food, but it is added to most water supplies in the United States.

Iodine. Iodine assists the thyroid gland in producing hormones. It is available in iodized salt and saltwater fish.

Iron. Commonly deficient in women, this mineral is essential for carrying oxygen in the blood. For women it is important to replenish supplies lost through menstruation. Iron determines how much oxygen moves through your blood to the cells. Fortunately, it is plentiful in lean red meats, chicken, fortified cereals, kidney beans, and lima beans.

Manganese. This mineral helps in the development of bones, teeth, and joints. It can be found in whole grain products, pineapple, and lentils.

Potassium. This mineral functions as an electrolyte and, along with sodium, moderates fluid balance and blood pressure. It is found in fruits, vegetables, and milk. Bananas, oranges, tomatoes, and peppers are especially good sources.

Selenium. Selenium is a mineral that works as an antioxidant. It can be found in seafood, liver, brown rice, and eggs.

Sodium. Because sodium is widely distributed in the food supply, it is not a problem to consume the minimum level of sodium needed. However, people who have a tendency toward high blood pressure need to moderate their intake of it. Sodium regulates blood pressure and muscle contraction. The major sources of sodium are table salt and the salt added to the food supply in processing.

Zinc. Zinc is very important for reproductive health in both men and women, skin health, and the immune system. It is available in beef, seafood, liver, eggs, and milk. Zinc is also present in wheat germ, but in a form that is less available to the body.

DO YOU NEED A VITAMIN & MINERAL SUPPLEMENT?

If you're not eating five servings of fruits and vegetables a day, do you need a vitamin pill? Many college students do take supplements. According to research by dietitian Nancie Herbold at Simmons College in Boston, teens are taking everything from vitamin C to gingko, but only 25 percent of those surveyed were getting advice on these products from a health professional (Herbold et al. 2004).

While most supplements like vitamin C and multivitamins are, at the very worst, a waste of money, others can be harmful. Supplements like androstenedione and growth hormones are extremely dangerous and should not be taken unless medical monitoring occurs. A study released by Wake Forest School of Medicine found that of 1,000 students surveyed, 3.5 percent reported using andro, 13.3 percent had tried creatine, and 2.5 percent had tried anabolic steroids (Kilgore 2000). The researchers found andro and creatine use was more common among athletes and weight lifters, and about one-third of andro users took anabolic steroids as well, a potentially lethal combination.

Teens often reported using supplements to promote weight loss or weight gain. For instance, 85 percent of overweight students in Herbold's study took supplements to help them shed pounds. About 3 percent of participants in Herbold's study were taking weight-loss products containing ephedra, a product the Food and Drug Administration says can cause severe cardiac side effects or even death in higher-than-recommended doses.

The reasons teens give for using supplements include good health, energy, bodybuilding, and weight loss. Teens even report that family, friends, physicians, and coaches introduced them to supplements. You should be particularly skeptical when merchants or store employees recommend a purchase; these people have a vested interest in your purchasing products!

Now that you know to stay away from those supplements we just discussed, we do feel comfortable recommending taking a multivitamin supplement for those times when you do not eat plenty of nutrient-dense foods. A multivitamin supplement that provides 100 percent of the daily requirement is like nutrition insurance. It can't hurt, and it can make up the difference when food intake doesn't meet your nutritional needs. Stick to multivitamins that give no more than 150 percent of the daily requirement. If the label shows 200 percent or more of the daily requirement for any nutrient, you should check with a physician.

Here is a list of common supplements that provide 100 percent of the daily requirement for vitamins and minerals for pennies a day:

Centrum—6 cents a day

Equate One—3 cents a day

One-A-Day for women or One-A-Day for men—
    7 cents a day

Spring Valley One Daily—4 cents a day

Diet Treatment for Colds & Flu

Jennifer is a freshman business major attending a state university. When interviewed about the quality of her diet, she said, "It's no wonder I got sick so often with all the animal crackers, popcorn, and mac 'n' cheese I put away."

While daily intake of fruits, vegetables, and a vitamin supplement can arm you with a powerful immune response to common viruses, the most important preventative measure against flu and colds is hand washing. This is especially true for people who live and work in public places—like college students who live in dorms and use public restrooms. Always wash your hands with hot water and soap after visiting a public place.

Since there is still no cure for the common cold, treatment has two goals: to relieve your stuffy head and achy body, and to help you fight off the virus to shorten the cold's duration. Lots of rest is the key. While fighting a stubborn infection, you may need twelve hours of sleep each night, so if at all possible, don't set that alarm. If not, aim to go to bed one hour early. You'll be most comfortable in a warm, humid environment. It's also important to drink lots of water. This promotes tissue healing, allows mucus to flow more freely, and helps with congestion.

No specific treatment exists for the virus that is causing your cold, but you can find some relief by treating your symptoms. For aches and pains accompanied by a fever of 100.5 degrees Fahrenheit or higher, take Tylenol or its generic equivalent. Always be sure to follow the directions on the package. If your throat is sore, gargle as often as you like with salt water (½ teaspoon salt in 1 cup of water).

Think twice before using heavily advertised over-the-counter cold and flu medications, which likely contain drugs for symptoms you don't have. Use of such products may result in needless overtreatment. Some of the drugs in these "cold pills" commonly induce drowsiness, making you feel worse.

Choosing good nutrition from foods on the A list will speed your recovery from a cold. Take your multivitamin to be sure your needs for vitamin A, the B complex vitamins, vitamin C, zinc, and copper are met. Both vitamin C and zinc boost the infection-fighting neutrophils, which fight colds at the cellular level.

While you have a cold, consider reducing your intake of dairy products; they can make mucus thicker. Chicken soup has been heralded as a cold therapy since the Middle Ages. Also, Asian healing treatments often use hot soups to treat upper respiratory infections, making use of chile peppers, lemongrass, and ginger in particular. Any food spicy enough to make your eyes water will have the same effect on your nose, promoting drainage. If you feel like eating a hot, spicy soup, it may help ease your symptoms. It may also interest you to know that recent scientific evidence shows mild support for the notion that chicken soup reduces cold symptoms, especially congestion (Rennard et al. 2000). Try the following recipe.

Chicken Soup in the Dorm

2 15-ounce cans chicken broth

1 10-ounce can white meat chicken

1 package instant ramen noodles plus the seasoning packet

Combine all of the ingredients in a large microwave-safe bowl and microwave on high power until boiling. Boil for 1 minute.

MORE REMEDIES TO EASE COLD SYMPTOMS

Essential oils may be rubbed on the body, inhaled with steam, diffused into the air, or poured on a cloth to be used as a compress. Try rubbing diluted eucalyptus oil on your chest as a decongestant, or inhale eucalyptus or peppermint oil to clear stuffiness. Adding a few drops of lavender, cedar, or lemon essential oil to a portable steamer or humidifier may also soothe nasal passages. Inhaling menthol not only provides relief from nasal congestion, but might help inhibit infection as well. Rosemary, thyme, mint, basil, and tea tree oils can also provide relief from symptoms of a cold. Use caution if you have asthma, since aromatherapy with essential oils can trigger an attack. Also, be sure never to ingest essential oils.

Echinacea may also help strengthen the immune system by stimulating the activity of white blood cells, but there is little evidence that it can prevent colds in particular. If you decide to try echinacea, take small doses for no more than eight weeks; prolonged use beyond this period of time may actually suppress your immune system.

Another herbal supplement with a strange name is astragalus. It is an inexpensive immune-enhancing herb that may help ward off flulike symptoms. Consider a brand like Nature's Way. You may also be interested in trying mushroom extract. An example of this type of product is Host Defense, an extract of seven mushrooms. It comes in an easy-to-swallow capsule form. As always with supplements, be sure to follow package directions; never take extra as a boost. Remember, when symptoms appear, continue taking a multivitamin—especially those with the antioxidant vitamins A, C, and E. These special nutrients play the role of circuit breaker at the cellular level. They insert themselves into the destructive chain of oxidative cellular events and halt molecular damage. It is believed that they also interrupt the aging process of cells.

Even though you can reduce your risk of illness with a multivitamin, the cold and flu organisms will always invade your dorm. One of the simplest and cheapest measures to combat these bugs is to choose immune-boosting foods such as 100 percent orange juice and other antioxidant-rich foods. Dietary prevention is also a cheaper strategy than expensive remedies. Orange juice is probably part of your cafeteria meal plan. Drink a six-ounce glass at least once a day. Here's a list of antioxidant-rich dorm foods:

- Strawberries
- Raspberries
- Oranges
- Dried apricots
- Apples
- Carrots
- Celery
- Soy nuts
- 100 percent orange or grapefruit juice

If you do get a flu, there is also no harm in trying an elderberry extract sold as Sambucol. It's used not for prevention, but for treatment. Studies from Israel indicate that Sambucol may make flu attacks less severe (Zakay-Rones et al. 1995). Yet another harmless and potentially effective cold treatment is to eat two to four cloves of raw garlic at the first sign of symptoms. It has to be raw garlic (found near the onions in the grocery store).

Keep in mind that these herbs may help alleviate symptoms; however, they should be taken with lots of water. Winter is a very dry time of year and if you live in a cold climate where indoor air is heated, moisture is sucked out of the air. This makes your mucous membranes dry so they fail to keep germs at bay. The solution is to drink a lot of water and put a humidifier (even if it is small) in your dorm room. If you're sick, add herbs or essential oils to the humidifier, such as eucalyptus, pine oil, thyme, and/or fenugreek. Essential oils can be poured onto a cotton ball and put near the steamer.

Finally, getting eight hours of sleep and washing your hands often are the best cost-free ways to combat the army of viruses hibernating in your dorm. If you end up buying over-the-counter remedies during your battle with a cold, you will end up spending at least three bucks a day. Stubborn colds can last for seven to ten days, and these costs can add up rapidly.

Thinking About Becoming a Vegetarian

Vegetarian foods are the source of nutrition for most of the world, and college is often the time when people in the United States begin to explore this food style. A vegetarian diet is healthy for people for all ages. In fact, it is believed that a vegetarian diet can protect people from both cancer and heart disease. There are three general classes of vegetarians:

- *Strict vegans* exclude all animal products, including meat, poultry, fish, eggs, and dairy products. Vegans eat fruits, vegetables, dried beans and peas (also known as legumes), grains, seeds and nuts.
- *Lacto vegetarians* exclude meat, poultry, fish, and eggs. They eat dairy foods in addition to fruits, vegetables, dried beans and peas, grains, seeds, and nuts.
- *Lacto-ovo vegetarian* is like lacto vegetarianism, except that eggs are also eaten.

Sometimes people experiment with vegetarianism by excluding red meat—pork, beef, veal, lamb, and so on. They may still eat chicken, turkey, fish, dairy products, and eggs, along with fruits, vegetables, dried beans and peas, grains, seeds, and nuts. All of these diets can promote optimal nutrition, and optimal cognitive and creative performance, if they are planned properly. The best way to ensure this is to eat a wide variety of foods. You may have heard about combining complementary protein foods in biology or nutrition class. It is not necessary to combine certain incomplete proteins during each and every meal (such as rice with beans), but it is important to eat a wide variety of foods at every meal so that all of the essential amino acids are available for manufacturing proteins. These are the repair and replacement nutrients that all the cells in your brain, nervous system, and immune system depend on. Proteins from plants can do the job if you concentrate on variety.

There are, however, several nutrients for vegetarians to monitor. For a strict vegan, it's difficult to consume enough calcium in food, and we recommend a supplement of at least 800 mg daily. Because iron, vitamin B_{12}, and vitamin D are a challenge to obtain when eating a vegetarian diet, we suggest a multivitamin supplement with 100 percent of all essential vitamins and minerals.

Low-Carbohydrate Diets

Anna is a freshman business major who tried the Atkins Diet during her freshman year at a state college. During the interview for this book, she said, "I gave it up. It just didn't work. And it took too long to cook healthy stuff. I ended up gaining weight."

While research has shown very low-carbohydrate diets (less than 30 grams daily) do not support long-term weight control, students sometimes decide they want to try this approach. While a low-carb diet may not be the right answer for the long haul, learning how many carbohydrates are found in sugary and starchy foods is a good strategy. Reducing calories and carbohydrates in your diet, especially from the refined flour and sugar in desserts and snacks, is an effective way to control weight. As an example, it's great to get to know how many carbs are in a cup of pasta compared to a cup of snap peas.

Be aware that a very low-carbohydrate diet could promote the blues for an already-stressed college student. A Massachusetts Institute of Technology study showed that carbohydrates boost the output of the neurotransmitter serotonin (Wurtman 1995). This is also known as the "happy brain chemical." Another way to put it is that carbohydrates are an edible tranquilizer. The bottom line is that every time you eat, you are feeding more than your stomach. You are feeding your brain and muscles, so include some carbohydrate from fruits, vegetables, low-fat milk, or whole grains at every meal.

What is a low-carb food? Food manufactures have added terms like "net carb," "effective carb," and "impact carb" to labels to give their products shelf appeal. The terms are not defined by the Food and Drug Administration, and in reality refer to the same thing. The "net carb" in a food is the difference between total carbohydrate and the grams of dietary fiber and sugar alcohol. The idea is that the body does not digest fiber, so calories from carbohydrate may be differentiated by their source: fiber, sugar, and starch. Limited amounts of sugar alcohols do not affect blood sugar, and so they are also subtracted from the total carbohydrate count to yield "effective carb" or "impact carb." The *Journal of the American Dietetic Association* guidelines (Marcason 2004) for persons counting carbohydrates for purposes of controlling diabetes differ from this market use of "net carb." The ADA allows half of the sugar alcohols to be subtracted, since about half are digested. Dietary fiber is subtracted from the total only if the fiber content is five or more grams per serving. The FDA is expected to offer official definitions of these terms in the future.

There is a better approach to weight loss than low-carb diets. Beyond choosing whole and colored foods from the A list and getting exercise daily, the best approach for weight loss in college is to seek the counsel of a registered dietitian (RD), who can personalize a plan that considers the food available to you, as well as your schedule, exercise needs, and environment. If concern about your weight is siphoning the mental energy you need for your studies, ask for a referral to an RD at your health services office.

When Thin Is Too Thin

Eating disorders affect 3 percent of all college students—more than any other age group (American Dietetic Association 1997). There are three types of eating disorders: anorexia nervosa, bulimia nervosa, and binge eating disorder. You may not realize it, but eating disorders actually stem from unresolved issues with self-esteem, self-expression, depression, power, and communication. Eating disorders are difficult to understand, treat, and cure. They often start when someone is dealing with a major loss in their life. These losses may include the death of a grandparent, a divorce in the family, or trouble in a personal relationship. The following are some signs that may indicate that someone you know is developing an eating disorder.

Signs of anorexia nervosa

- Extremely thin
- Rapid weight loss
- Loss of menstrual periods
- Fine hair on arms, legs, and face
- Frequent complaints of nausea, bloating, or constipation
- Rigidly avoiding certain foods
- Obsessing about food but not eating
- Exercising excessively
- Feeling fat even when very thin
- Socially withdrawn
- Refusal to admit eating pattern is abnormal

Signs of bulimia nervosa

- Onset often occurring after weight loss
- Usually near ideal body weight, but with fluctuations
- Eats large meals without gaining weight
- Dental enamel erosion
- Swollen cheeks
- Irregular menstrual periods
- Binge eating (episodes of uncontrolled consumption)
- Leaving to go the bathroom after eating
- Using laxatives or diuretics
- Hiding eating from others

Signs of binge eating disorder

- Forcing vomiting or diarrhea to purge body of food
- Usually overweight or obese
- Frequent attempts to diet
- Losing and regaining weight often
- Binge eating or eating when not hungry
- Eating to the point of extreme pain
- Eating large amounts of food in a short time
- Feeling out of control when eating and unable to stop
- Realizing that eating patterns are abnormal

While anorexia and bulimia are medical diagnoses, the term *disordered eating* is used to describe someone who has a troubled relationship with food and eating.

Signs of disordered eating

- Eating when not hungry
- Not eating when feeling hungry
- Feeling guilty about eating
- Avoiding certain foods or large categories of foods
- Hiding eating from others

If you have a concern about someone who may exhibit any of these signs, remember, the sooner the person gets help, the better. No one has to face or treat an eating disorder alone. The first step should be to talk with a doctor, nurse, counselor, or dietitian. Counseling is always a part of the treatment. There are support groups on many college campuses. If you have a friend who is battling an eating disorder, you can help by being a good listener and caring for and encouraging your friend. Do not be judgmental, criticize, or try to police the person's eating. Those strategies can simply add to his or her feeling of lacking control. Recovery takes a long time and is a lifetime effort. Success does not come overnight. The disorder is not cured when symptoms are no longer visible. The person is always at risk of relapse. The faster he or she gets help, the greater the chance for a full recovery to normalized relationships and healthy eating.

Places to Find Help with Nutrition Concerns

This book has given you some background information on nutrition, but if you still have questions, or if you have special concerns, there are several campus resources you can consult.

College food or health services office. A registered dietitian is usually available through the residence life department at large universities to counsel students with dietary concerns. Whether you're concerned about food allergy or controlling diabetes, most college health services offices will be able to link you to a nutrition professional for wise guidance.

Wellness houses. If eating right is important to you, ask about living on a wellness floor or in a wellness house. If your school offers this option, you can choose to live with others who are personally committed to a healthy lifestyle. Having a roommate or housemate who supports and lives a healthy lifestyle can make all the difference.

Support groups. Your college may host a Weight Watchers chapter or a support group for students who are dealing with eating disorders. Look on the cafeteria bulletin board or visit the health services office to find out where people meet to talk about food and nutrition issues. Find additional support through your residence advisor.

Become an advocate for change on your campus. College food service professionals are always looking for ways to meet the needs of their customers. Many are also responding in creative ways to the freshman fifteen. Make sure to check out the labels of cafeteria selections. They may identify items as low-fat or low-carbohydrate. Along with the ABC ratings found in this book, you can use cafeteria labels in your decision process. If your school does not offer a salad bar, low-fat dairy choices, fresh fruits, and grilled entrées, it may be time to make an appointment with someone in the residence life or food services department. These are the places to start to learn about your choices for healthy eating and advocate your important viewpoint to the policy makers. Or you can write a letter to the editor of your student newspaper, demanding, "Where are my vitamins and minerals?" Doing so always brings a response.

What You Need to Know About Alcohol

During your college experience, you will become of legal age to drink beer, wine, and hard liquor. The relationship of alcohol to health is a complicated subject, and one that you have probably started to sort out. Use the following general guidelines to evaluate your unique and individual relationship with alcohol. Whether you abstain or want to have beer every time you eat pizza, consider these benchmarks.

Moderate intake of one serving daily for women and one to two servings daily for men seems to produce a health benefit. You may have heard of the Mediterranean diet and the French paradox. Whether due to the antioxidants in wine or its relaxation effect, there is a documented health benefit for moderate intake of one drink for women and one or two for men daily. What is a serving? It is twelve ounces of beer, five ounces of wine, or one ounce of hard liquor such as vodka, whiskey, or scotch.

But please remember this: Alcohol intake above those levels (one serving for women and up to two for men) impairs your physical and emotional health. In college, if you are tired all the time or catching every little sniffle or sore throat that comes along, ask yourself if alcohol is part of the problem. If it is, follow the rule of one for women, two for men. And if you can't seem to control how much you drink or you wake up from a fitful sleep feeling guilty about how much you drank the night before, talk to someone about it. Talk to a friend or trusted family member, your resident advisor, or someone at the health services office. You should be especially careful if you know there is a history of substance abuse in your family. Alcohol is an important adult issue you will have to learn about in college. Of course, if there is any chance that you are pregnant, you should strictly avoid alcohol consumption.

Responsible colleges and universities offer help to students who have problems with alcohol or drugs. For example, at one Big Ten university, a free confidential program is available to assist students who want to talk about their problems with alcohol or other drugs. The major purpose is to help students remain healthy in school so they can reach their academic goals.

Services at college alcohol assistance centers may include interventions and support groups. Intervention is an assessment that begins with an interview between a counselor and student. Together they determine what role alcohol or other drugs play in the student's life. Next, the counselor discusses options the student may wish to pursue. These may include participation in an education series, short-term outpatient treatment, or a continuing-care support group.

A support group may be a good way to confront the ongoing challenge of alcohol and drugs in college. Normally, a substance abuse counselor facilitates discussion among group members about the impact of the substance in their lives. Students collectively explore options and make decisions about their future use. Students may use alcohol to cope with problems in their lives, such as the death of a family member or the breakup of a relationship. If the use of alcohol or drugs starts to impact your physical, emotional, or academic well-being or the health of someone you care about, it is time to talk to a professional.

About Marijuana & Uncontrolled Eating

Marijuana is the most widely used illicit drug among college youth today and is more potent than ever. Marijuana use can lead to a host of significant health, social, learning, and behavioral problems at a crucial time in a college student's development. Getting high also impairs judgment, which can lead to overeating, as well as truly risky decisions like having sex, shoplifting, or riding in a vehicle with someone who is under the influence of drugs or alcohol. According to the National Center on Addiction and Substance Abuse at Columbia University, teens who use drugs are five times more likely to have sex than teens who do not use drugs (Califano 2004). Sexual encounters, in turn, can lead to pregnancy or transmission of sexual diseases. Getting high also contributes to general apathy, irresponsible behavior, and risky choices.

The use of marijuana correlates with uncontrolled eating and subsequent weight gain. A powerful urge to eat after smoking pot is now clearly understood by scientists. Getting high and experiencing "the munchies"—which can lead to eating whole bags of sandwich cookies or an entire half gallon of ice cream straight from the carton—is caused by THC (delta-9-tetrahydrocannabinol), the active chemical ingredient in marijuana. Scientists have also discovered that compounds related to the active ingredient in cannabis occur naturally in the body and play an important role in regulating appetite. Smoking a joint actually masks a person's natural appetite suppressors.

Don't be fooled by popular beliefs. Research shows that marijuana leads to both weight gain and addiction. The users you see on campus, the "stoners"—well, they won't admit it, but they are hooked on pot. Each year, more students enter treatment with a primary diagnosis of marijuana dependence than for all other illicit drugs combined (Califano 2004).

Usually smoked as a cigarette or joint, or in a pipe or bong, marijuana has appeared in "blunts" in recent years. These are cigars that have been emptied of tobacco and refilled with marijuana. Some users also mix marijuana into foods or use it to brew tea.

Research shows (Califano 2004) that students who smoke marijuana engage in risky behaviors that can jeopardize their future, like having sex, getting in trouble with the law, or losing scholarship funding. Marijuana hurts academic achievement and puts young adults at risk for depression and anxiety. Short-term effects of marijuana use include problems with memory and learning, distorted perception (such as not experiencing feelings of stomach fullness), difficulty in thinking and problem solving, loss of coordination, and increased heart rate, anxiety, and panic attacks.

Researchers have found that marijuana's active ingredient, THC, changes the way in which sensory information gets into and is acted on by the part of the brain called the *hippocampus* (Pope and Yergelun-Todd 1996). This component of the brain's limbic system is crucial for learning, memory, and the integration of sensory experiences with emotions and motivations. Investigations have shown that THC suppresses neurons in the information-processing system of the hippocampus. In addition, researchers have discovered that learned behaviors, which depend on the hippocampus, also deteriorate (Pope and Yergelun-Todd 1996).

You may not know that someone who smokes marijuana regularly may also have many of the same respiratory problems that tobacco smokers have. These individuals may have daily cough and phlegm, symptoms of chronic bronchitis, and frequent chest colds. Continuing to smoke marijuana can lead to abnormal functioning of lung tissue that has been injured or destroyed by marijuana smoke.

Regardless of the THC content, the amount of tar inhaled by marijuana smokers and the level of carbon monoxide absorbed are three to five times greater than among tobacco smokers. This may be related to the fact that marijuana users inhale deeply and hold the smoke in their lungs.

A study of college students has shown that critical skills related to attention, memory, and learning are impaired among people who use marijuana heavily, even after discontinuation of use for at least twenty-four hours (Pope and Yergelun-Todd 1996). Researchers compared sixty-five heavy users, who had smoked marijuana an average of twenty-nine out of thirty days, with sixty-four light users, who had smoked an average of one out of thirty days. After a nineteen- to twenty-four-hour period of abstinence from marijuana and other illicit drugs and alcohol, researchers evaluated the undergraduates' attention, memory, and learning. Compared to the light users, heavy marijuana users made more errors and had more difficulty sustaining attention, shifting attention to meet changes in the environment, and registering, processing, and using information. These findings suggest that greater impairment among heavy users is likely to result from an alteration of brain activity produced by marijuana.

If you know marijuana use is the reason you flubbed a chemistry quiz or spaced out during a Microeconomics assignment, then it is time to be honest with yourself. Is academic success and a meaningful career more important to you than an occasional high? Talk with someone you trust about how you are going to give up marijuana or start with a visit to the campus counseling center.

Food Allergies

The most common food allergens are peanuts, walnuts, pecans, almonds, dairy products, eggs, soy products, wheat, fish, and shellfish. Up to 8 percent of college students may have food allergies (National Institute of Allergy and Infectious Diseases 2005). While the rate of peanut allergy seems to be increasing, milk and egg allergies actually affect more students. A true food allergy, as opposed to a food intolerance, occurs when the immune system mistakenly interprets something in a food as an invader. The body then produces antibodies to fight it. When this happens repeatedly, the defense response includes the release of histamine and other powerful chemicals. Symptoms of this allergic response can include itchy mouth, itchy tongue, and hives. Severe symptoms are also possible, including an inability to breathe, shock, and cardiac arrest. Students with severe allergies often carry a dose of prescription epinephrine with them at all times. Epinephrine is the treatment for the most severe allergic response.

Food Triggers for Migraine Headaches

Migraine is a condition characterized by severe head pain plus one or more other symptoms such as an upset stomach, vomiting, or sensitivity to light, sound, or smell. A migraine headache can last anywhere between half a day and up to three days. Students who experience migraines have to put their lives on hold until the headache goes away. There are diet factors that can trigger migraines (American Dietetic Association Foundation 1995). Ignoring hunger and skipping meals have also been known to trigger headaches. Here are some common food triggers for migraines:

- Red wine, vermouth, champagne, and beer
- Coffee, tea, and soft drinks
- Aged cheeses, such as Cheddar
- Sourdough and homemade bread
- Some types of beans, including broad, Italian, lima, lentil, and soy
- Vegetables, including sauerkraut, peas, and avocados
- Peanuts and peanut butter
- Cured meats, such as ham, corned beef, sausage, bacon, and lunch meat
- Pickled herring and chicken liver
- Canned soup or soup made from mixes
- Chocolate desserts
- Overripe bananas
- Any food with monosodium glutamate (MSG)—found in Chinese foods, barbecue sauces, soy sauce, marinades, and meat tenderizers

keeping fit no matter how busy you get

Here comes a chapter you might not want to read. It would be nice if you could control your weight and stay fit with the food lists in chapter 1 and the awesome recipes in chapter 2. But there is more to this fitness program than eating right. You're probably saying to yourself, "Keeping fit? No problem. I managed to stay in shape in high school, and I was always rushed. Why should college be any different?"

Well, because it is. Even if you're eating all the right foods from the A list, exercise needs to be part of your college life. But it isn't easy. Amanda, a freshman going to a private liberal arts college where she is majoring in nursing, said, "Thankfully, I walk a lot back and forth to classes, because I don't have time to exercise. My friends will say, 'You wanna walk?' But by the time I'm all done with my work, it's dark."

And, according to a published study (Chakravarthy, Joyner, and Booth 2002), Amanda's exercise pattern is normal:

- Nearly half of young people aged twelve to twenty-one are not vigorously active on a regular basis.
- Physical activity declines dramatically with age during adolescence.
- Female adolescents are much less physically active than male adolescents.

Reasons Students Struggle to Keep Fit

Every one of the students we surveyed said they struggled with weight gain during their freshman year. Some of these students were extremely active, in the "busy" sense of active. They were on the go, running from class to work to meetings, just as they were in high school. Others were football players, tennis stars, and swimmers on hardworking teams, practicing every day.

It is a common struggle to keep a college waistline from expanding. There are many reasons why. Here are some of the common ones uncovered in our interviews.

THIS ISN'T HIGH SCHOOL

Let's face it: you probably hated climbing the rope or running the mile in high school gym class, but it kept you in shape. If nothing else, it usually meant that you were getting outdoors and moving your body for a sufficient period of time. Many high school students participate in team sports during high school. Whether that sport is football or dance, it gives you the opportunity to be physical. When you start college, you may lose that regular workout. You aren't having basketball practice every day. That PE teacher is not there yelling to get moving. For many students, this loss of activity creeps up on them before they realize it. One day you realize you've been putting on the pounds. A big part of the reason is because you've settled into a routine without regular exercise.

NOT ENOUGH TIME

You don't need to train for the Olympics to feel fit, but time is not on your side in college. You are going to feel busier than you were in high school, but everyone has at least a half hour to spare on most days. Thirty minutes of brisk activity five days a week is widely recommended by health care professionals. Every student that we surveyed had this much time. As you plan your class schedule, consider a personal fitness class. This is just one way to build physical activity into your college life. But, there is another problem . . .

LOW MOTIVATION

As your mother might say, "laziness." In this new world of college, you will be working very hard to keep up with your Politics of War and Peace class, physics lab assignments, and math study groups. You might be participating in a choir or in student government. When you get back to your dorm room after a busy day, you are going to want to put your feet up, turn on the TV and relax, whether the day was really challenging or downright easy. That's okay. But the habit you want to work toward is to combine at least thirty minutes of physical activity with a TV break.

Our visits with students revealed that most struggled to keep fit because of these two reasons: time and motivation. These are factors that will continue to complicate your exercise habits through college and into adult life. In this chapter, you will hear from two experts who are going to help convince you, once and for all, of the powerful benefits of exercise. First, a physical therapist will explain the science of aerobic exercise. Later, a scientist from Yale University Hospital will explain the research behind the super six-minute workout. The freshman fifteen doesn't have to refer to weight gain, and this chapter will prove it by offering you fifteen creative, inexpensive, and fun ways to keep active. For now, let's discuss why it is so important to your college success for you to be active.

Ten Benefits of Physical Activity

To understand the benefits of physical activity during your late teens and early twenties, read what Carolyn Hoffmann, a licensed physical therapist, has to say. Hoffmann has a BS in physical therapy and has been helping people find ways to keep fit for nearly twenty-seven years. She has faithfully exercised since her days at Washington University in St. Louis. Carolyn is also the mother of a college junior and a college-bound high school junior. She identified the ten benefits of physical activity that students know and care about most (Hoffman 2004).

1. Improves self-esteem. You just feel taller and stronger walking out of the gym after a workout. Physical fitness is a value of our culture and translates into improved self-esteem.

2. Assists in weight control. Physical exercise helps you maintain a healthy weight. Don't equate an aerobic exercise class with pounds dropped on a scale, because many people gain weight as they turn flab into muscle. Rather, exercise is a way to manage your weight over the long term, because muscle cells continually twitch and burn more calories in comparison to fat cells. Exercise is more like an insurance policy to guard against weight gain in college.

3. Sharpens your mind and assists in staying on task. The increased blood flow from exercise helps keep your brain infused with oxygen so your mind stays sharp in the classroom. The enhanced feeling of alertness helps you become more productive overall.

4. Improves flexibility, strength, and endurance. After a half hour of brisk walking, you aren't thinking about flexibility, strength, and endurance, but these benefits are just as important as building muscles. With lifelong use of all your muscles, you may avoid many degenerative conditions, like joint pain, later in life.

5. Reenergizes a person. Exercise keeps your insulin regulated, helping you to avoid hyper highs and jittery lows.

6. Produces endorphins. On the science side of things, exercise creates many good feelings. Exercise will produce endorphins, which make you feel upbeat. Endorphins also decrease whatever pain your body may be feeling, much like a natural ibuprofen.

7. Improves calm and reduces anxiety. Moving your arms and legs in a game of flag football or on the elliptical machine at the gym helps reduce stress because you have your mind on something else, and it gives you a break from the issue or environment that is your stressor.

8. Promotes good sleep. Exercise produces what some people call "that good feeling of being tired." After exercise, your muscles crave rest, and you won't be tossing and turning all night.

9. Decreases fatigue. Exercise, combined with proper stretching, decreases the amount of lactic acid in your body. Lactic acid contributes to fatigue and muscle soreness. Stretching can help you break down lactic acid and reduce the feelings of fatigue and soreness. Consequently, you will feel better, longer.

10. Prevents disease and illness. Exercise can help you stay disease free by "working out" the bugs that infest your body. During cold and flu season, a regular game of volleyball can help keep you strong to fight off disease organisms in your dorm.

Walking—A Good Start

As mentioned before, beginning an exercise program does not immediately translate into pounds lost on a scale. Rather, your new habit of being active will likely show up first as a feeling of well-being. The weight loss will follow.

And you don't have to run a marathon the first week to achieve this weight loss. Rather, to lose weight, you can start slow and easy; then, you continually build up your distance, resistance, and pace. For example, you can get out of your dorm right now and walk—just ten minutes—even if you aren't used to it. Tomorrow, you can walk ten minutes but take the hilly route. You'll be increasing your resistance. Think about investing in a pedometer to keep track of your steps. This small device keeps track of your distance throughout the day and costs only about ten to fifteen dollars. It might actually be fun to build extra steps into your walks and your daily routine around the dorm. As you keep taking walks, build up the duration to fifteen minutes, then twenty, and quicken the pace. Do it gradually—but don't quit moving. Walking is great for weight loss because it burns calories, it's easy, and it is by far the least expensive activity you can do.

America On the Move is a national initiative to encourage walking. It was started by Dr. James Hill of Denver, Colorado, in 2004. A deceptively simple strategy, the idea is to wear a pedometer and take more steps today than you did the day before, with the goal of increasing your movement by two thousand steps, or about one mile. This is the equivalent of 100 calories, or one pound lost per month. With chapters in twenty states, you may want to register as a member at www.americaonthemove.org.

Counting steps instead of miles can also boost your workout. Researchers in England asked twelve women to climb a two-hundred-step staircase, progressing from once a day to six times a day (Boreham et al. 2005). Each ascent took about two minutes, so by the end of this study, the women were exercising twelve minutes each. In less than two months, they saw a boost in their fitness level, along with improvements in their

Aaron, who is undecided about his major: *It took me a couple days to get out of my laziness and make it down to the gym. Once I did, it made me feel like I had accomplished something. This one-hour-a-day exercise plan has helped me feel more active so far. It really helped me get out of the lazy feeling that I had when I wasn't working out. I have discovered that I need to keep working out because it is very easy to lose motivation if you skip a day. I have been mixing it up with playing soccer and some basketball.*

cholesterol level. This study shows that even short bouts of exercise can have a tremendous benefit.

You may hear many different terms to describe variations of walking, like *power walking* and *race walking*. In all cases, posture is very important to avoid back discomfort. When walking, the spine should be stretched upward in a straight yet relaxed position. To avoid swayback, it also helps to hold your stomach muscles in and, at the same time, tuck your buttocks under your body. Relax your shoulders and allow your arms to swing freely. Bend your arms at the elbows to burn 5 to 10 percent more calories while walking (Spilner 2001).

TWICE THE BURN

To take your walking to the next level, consider hill or stair walking. Trekking up and down hills, a 150-pound student burns 400 calories per hour. Walking the stairs can burn up to 600 calories per hour (Spilner 2001).

CHOOSING WALKING SHOES

Having given some thought to your form, now all you need is a comfortable pair of shoes! Comfortable shoes will help protect you from developing painful foot conditions. Walkers should consider the following when purchasing a pair of athletic shoes:

Fit. Size both feet and fit to the larger one. Allow one thumb width between your longest toe and the end of the shoe. Look for a low, supportive heel that has a rounded shape at the bottom, rather than being flared out. A thick heel or one that flares out will cause your foot to slap down rather than roll. This may contribute to sore shins. Be sure the sole is flexible. You should be able to twist and bend the toe area.

Support. Choose a shoe that matches your arch. The shoe should be lightweight and made of breathable material.

Cushioning. Coming mainly from the midsole, cushioning disperses force as the foot contacts the ground.

RESISTANCE & PACE

To add resistance to your walking workout, consider wearing a weighted vest. We prefer a vest instead of wrist or ankle weights to avoid undue stress on particular joints. To add variety to your walking routine, try skipping, high stepping, walking backward, or hopping. All of these variations use leg muscles in different ways. Soon you will be in the routine of walking briskly for exercise, and you will miss it when there's a rainstorm or you don't have time. What's the next step after walking? You need not run a marathon, but why not challenge yourself to a simple running program, like twenty to thirty minutes daily? Walking is a good start, especially for students who carry extra weight. But if you can run, run. One way to start is to jog at intervals during your walk. The faster your pace, the more likely you are to achieve aerobic benefits.

Aerobic Exercise Boosts Your Energy Level

Running is an example of an activity that provides a cardiovascular or aerobic workout, because it elevates your heart rate. To achieve aerobic benefits, you must elevate your heart rate by twenty beats per minute over your baseline or resting rate (National Center for Chronic Disease Prevention and Health Promotion 1999). Aerobic activities get your heart pumping and build up endorphins, which you may recall are the "natural happy chemicals."

Aerobic exercise includes very brisk walking and running, as well as basketball, bicycling, aerobic dancing, tennis, rope jumping, soccer, and swimming. Aerobic exercises can be used to boost your energy level at the time you need it most. If you have class late in the morning, you might want to do your exercise first thing in the morning. Place your exercise clothes and shoes right next to the alarm clock or radio. That will be your reminder to get going. Or if you intend to exercise right after class is over in the afternoon, place your clothes on the desk chair. It will be a visible reminder when you walk back into the room.

To get started right now, set aside one hour a day for your choice of aerobic activity. This can be a group activity, like soccer, or your own version of jog-walking. Use the first fifteen minutes to stretch and warm up. Then go at it—at full pace—for a half hour. Use the last fifteen minutes to cool down.

Building Strength

We know you will feel better both instantly and over the long term by getting off your duff and elevating your heart rate. But what if you want to build strength? Experts agree that to build strength, you need to work all your muscle groups; not just your arms, legs, and chest. Too many people go into the weight room and try to do as many bench presses as they can. You need to work all of the muscle groups in your body, or you will compromise balance and coordination. Working to build strength along with a core strength/stretching program like yoga or Pilates is the best approach. Again, if you do only heavy lifting in order to build muscle, you could experience a weight gain. This bothers some people who are lifting in order to lose weight, but since muscle weighs more than fat, muscle weight gain is difficult to avoid.

Begin slowly by selecting a lower weight that you can lift with a little resistance, and work on repetition. This might be ten pounds on the upper arm machine or twenty pounds on the overhead pull.

A SIMPLE SIX-WEEK STRENGTH- BUILDING PROGRAM

Here is an example of a starter program for three days a week. Commit yourself to this for six weeks. You should arrive at your workouts feeling strong and refreshed. If not, you may be overtraining. Keep in mind, you need to have rest days between bodybuilding workouts. Since your body grows during rest days, not training days, you need to give it enough time to recover.

Day one: Chest (bench press with bar or dumbbell press, flyes, push-ups); triceps (bench dips, kickbacks)

Day two: Back (bent-over rows); biceps (curls, standing or seated)

Brandon, a music major from Minnesota: *It is hard to find time each day to exercise. I have been able to exercise more than usual, which is great, because when I do get the chance, I feel better about myself. I have more motivation to go again and I sleep better.*

Darius, who is studying political science: *I feel I am better able to deal with stress when I am exercising every day. Whether it is playing basketball, soccer, walking, jogging, or running, I really feel better about myself. Even if I struggle with my diet, I feel I can overcome it with the amount of exercise I do every day.*

Day three: Shoulders (lateral raises, front raises), legs (squats, lunges)

For each exercise, do ten to twelve repetitions and one to three sets. You will need to start by selecting a weight you can lift ten to twelve times with consistency. When you can easily lift the weight twelve times, increase the weight. You can also use this variation:

Day one: Chest (bench press with bar or dumbbell press, flyes, push-ups); back (bent-over rows, pull-downs)

Day two: Biceps (curls, standing or seated); triceps (bench dips, kickbacks)

Day three: Shoulders (lateral raises, front raises); legs (squats, lunges)

You will notice results from this six-week program in just a week. In one month, you will feel and look stronger. At the end of six weeks, evaluate your progress and celebrate. Then decide if you want to maintain your fitness level or increase it by increasing your time, repetitions, or weights. In general, the more weight you press, the bigger your muscles. The more repetitions you do (at lower weights), the more toned your muscles.

How About Swimming?

Some people just don't want to pump iron. An alternative for both cardiovascular health and strength building is a progressive swimming program. Why is water exercise so popular and beneficial? Water offers more resistance to movement than air does. When you push against the water with low force, you receive low resistance from the water. As you build up your strength and push with higher force against the water, you encounter higher resistance. For this reason, water exercise is very efficient. It is also the treatment of choice for injured athletes. Swimming does not have to be monotonous either. If you become bored with the crawl, switch to breaststroke or sidestroke. Here's an example of a progressive swimming program:

Week One

Day one: Swim six minutes, any stroke with easy effort

Day two: Swim eight minutes, any stroke with easy effort

Day three: Swim ten minutes, any stroke with easy effort

Week Two

All three days: Swim ten minutes, any stroke with easy effort. Rest two minutes. Swim four minutes, any stroke with easy effort.

Week Three

All three days: Add two minutes to your second swim for a total of six minutes.

Week Four

All three days: Add two more minutes to your second swim for a total of eight minutes.

Week Five

All three days: Add two more minutes to your second swim for a total of ten minutes.

Week Six

All three days: Rest after the second ten-minute swim, then swim for two more minutes.

Weeks Seven and On

All three days: Keep adding two more minutes to your third swimming session, building up to ten minutes (or thirty minutes total) with short rests between the three ten-minute sets.

Water exercise can be addictive. Go online to find out when your campus pool is scheduled for open lap swimming. Rummage in that bottom drawer for your suit or trunks and get started. Don't forget to locate the clock before you dive in. Starting out with six minutes of movement is your victory for day one.

The Six-Minute Workout

Don't have twenty minutes for an aerobic dance tape? Studies at Yale University's School of Medicine are measuring the effectiveness of a simple six-minute workout. Geoff Twohill, an expert in occupational therapy at Yale-New Haven Hospital, says the idea is based on combining the effects of both aerobic and anaerobic activities:

Aerobic exercise is longer-duration exercise, targeting slow-twitch muscle groups. It also requires oxygen to burn fat. Walking and jogging are examples.

Anaerobic exercise is of shorter duration and features resistance. It targets fast-twitch muscle groups and requires little oxygen to burn calories. As anaerobic activity switches to aerobic activity during intense but prolonged muscular work (as in a six-minute bout), oxygen enters muscle cells and promotes the burning of fat in addition to carbohydrate. Combining intense work with prolonged duration is the most efficient way to burn the most calories. You already know that burning more calories than you eat equals weight loss, so consider the six-minute-workout part of your dorm room life.

The six-minute-workout is a simple, time-effective workout routine combining the calorie-burning capabilities of aerobic exercise with a focus on trunk musculature and endurance to tap into the benefits of those oxygen-dependent slow-twitch groups. In a nutshell, all of the above means that hard work in short bursts can be as effective as a lot of work over a longer time, if you do it correctly. The program consists of four exercises, each done in three consecutive sets, for a total of six minutes:

- Push-ups: as many as possible for twenty seconds, all of similar quality.

Robin, a student who goes to the gym regularly: *The six- minute-workout gets two thumbs up!*

Sean, a student who almost lives in the science lab: *The six-minute-workout has been going well. I think the fact that it only takes six minutes and that you can do it in your dorm room makes it an ideal solution for college kids. I have not found it to be too strenuous at all, but I have definitely felt a difference, especially with the sit-ups.*

- Rest for ten seconds, then repeat the exercise-resting pattern two more times, for a total of one and a half minutes used.
- Immediately follow this procedure with standing deep knee squats, with the same exercise- resting pattern.
- Follow with stomach crunches, again in the same pattern. Lie flat, with your knees bent. Put your hands behind your head and come up slowly, touching your elbows to your knees. Do as many as you can for twenty seconds, then rest for ten. Repeat crunches and rest two more times for a total of a minute and a half.
- Finish with pull-ups/chin-ups, again in the same pattern. If you are in the dorm, you can use a high bunk bed frame or the top of a door to pull yourself up. Do twenty seconds of pull-ups, ten seconds of rest. Repeat this two more times.

This workout will total an exhausting six minutes! You will have worked all of the core muscles of your body in this time, and taken next to no time out of your day to do it.

Our study's early results with people who have used this routine show significant changes in body fat percentage and strength. The key to this is maintaining the intensity of the workout. Since you will only be working for six minutes, you can't afford to take a longer break than normal, or the workout will lose its effectiveness. The routine is called *closed chain*, a term that refers to the use of trunk muscles to stabilize the body throughout each exercise. The theory is that you first utilize the anaerobic capabilities of the muscles to initiate an efficient burn of calories, continue to burn fat as your supply of oxygen is restored during your chosen cooldown routine, such as stretching.

The "fad" here is that it's not time-consuming, and most importantly for the participant, it works.

Tips on Staying Motivated

So far, we've talked about walking, running, weight lifting, swimming, and a quick all-purpose workout. But how do you get started with any of these programs?

As soon as you get to college, go out and introduce yourself to at least three people. The next day, meet one more new person. Within this growing group, find someone who is also physically active or possibly even has the same ideas and goals for fitness as you do. The two of you can establish a plan for keeping healthy and active, whether it's walking together, playing Frisbee, or shooting hoops. Once you establish the plan, stick to it! When you are exercising with someone else, it's okay if a little competitiveness settles in—it will keep you motivated and add to the fun.

On the other hand, if you're more comfortable exercising alone and need motivation, set little goals for yourself. Huge looming goals are difficult because you don't see progress right away. Many of us are in the instant gratification mind-set. If your goal is to lose weight, don't set some huge number like fifty pounds. Start with a smaller number, like ten pounds. That number equals one size down in blue jeans. Once you achieve that weight goal, celebrate. Take time to feel your success before deciding if you want or need to lose more. It's frustrating, if not impossible, to motivate yourself when your goal seems far away. By having a series of little goals instead of one large one, you give yourself little victories along the way. By starting slowly, you will avoid disappointment, as well as injury. After all, you can't just walk into the gym and bench-press three hundred pounds—it takes time. And consider consulting a trainer at the college gym or joining a weight-control support group to share ideas for meeting your fitness and weight goals.

Even if you are keeping active with solo activities, it's a good idea to inform other people, such as friends and family, of your goals. Having other people informed will help keep you honest about meeting your goals and fan your desire to achieve them. For example, if you're trying to lose weight and it's going to rain all weekend, you're going to have to find an indoor activity that keeps you on track. Telling the people you are closest to about your goals will keep you focused. Moral support makes any task easier.

It comes down to this in the end: You have to want to be an active person for the long haul. You have to want personal fitness enough to get through the first few weeks of discomfort. And you can't just do it for someone else. Doing something for someone else, whether it is building strength or losing weight, isn't going to work in the long run. But if it's something you want to do to make yourself feel good, there is nothing stopping you!

Measuring Calories Burned with Exercise

Now that you've decided to get moving, you probably want to know exactly what you're losing. What you generally want to use and lose are stored calories. Calories are stored when you don't burn up what you ate that day. All activities burn calories. Most foods have calories. Some foods, like a candy bar milk shake, have a lot of calories, while others, such as a bowl of strawberries, don't have many. That's one reason strawberries are on the A list and milk shakes are not. But we are talking about activity here.

To determine the number of calories you are expending from an activity, you first need to learn your body weight in kilograms (kg). You can determine your weight in kilograms by dividing your weight in pounds by 2.2. For example, if you weigh 150 pounds, your weight in kilograms is 68. Once you've found your weight in kilograms, multiply it by the metabolic equivant (MET) value in the table on the next page. METs are a measure of how much energy you will expend doing the activity. Once you have the product of your weight in kilograms and the MET value, you multiply this value by the time spent in hours. Let's take light biking as an example:

The MET is 6. So 68 kg. times 6 METs equals 408.

Then multiply the product, 408, by the hours of activity.

Let me explain: If you bike at a light pace for 45 minutes, that's .75 hour.

So you would multiply 408 by .75 to find that you burn 306 calories for this activity.

Is Algebra I coming back to you? Here is another example:

You weigh 180 pounds and you practice yoga on videotape in your dorm for 40 minutes.

Your weight in kilograms is 180 pounds divided by 2.2, or 82. The MET for yoga is 4.

So 81 kg x 4 METs x .66 hours equals 216 calories.

So, you have expended 216 calories in 40 minutes by stretching and bending in your dorm room. Here are some METs for common activities (Ainsworth et al. 1993):

MET for Common College Activities

Activity	MET Value
Biking leisurely	4
Biking lightly, 10-12 mph	6
Biking moderately, 12-14 mph	8
Biking vigorously, 14-16 mph	10
Biking (racing), 16-19 mph	12
Biking (racing), 20+ mph	16
Circuit resistance training	8
Resistance training, light	3
Resistance training, vigorous	6
Stretching, yoga	4
Water aerobics	4
Golf	4.5
Tennis	7
Walking, very slow	2
Walking, slow	2.5
Walking, normal	3
Walking, moderate	3.5
Walking, brisk	4
Walking, uphill	6
Aerobics	6
Jogging	7

Running, 12-minute mile	8
Running, 10-minute mile	10
Running, 8.5-minute mile	11.5
Running, 7.5-minute mile	13.5
Running, 6.5-minute mile	15
Running, 5.5-minute mile	18
Running, cross-country	9
Running, up stairs	15
Swimming, laps	10
Skiing	7
Calisthenics (push-ups, sit-ups) vigorous	8

These exercises are the most common ways to keep active and fit. But don't rule out horseback riding or Frisbee golf. Because if you don't find some way to stay active, you could very well become a statistic.

Ways to Keep Moving & Have Fun

Yes, the fear of the freshman fifteen is real for any college student. It is more acute for the student who is especially image conscious about his or her body. The lists and tips and recipes you found at the beginning of this book are going to help. At this point, it doesn't hurt to point out that alcohol is a major contributor to weight gain. With seven nutrient-empty calories per gram, beer and wine coolers get deposited directly on the hips and stomach. Let's face it, you also eat a lot of junk late at night while you're woozy from booze. The good news is that you can avoid gaining any weight if you make and stick with a few decisions about your schedule and lifestyle at the very start of the year. There are smarter things to do with your time and brain cells than getting wasted. Not only will these suggestions be helpful, but most of them are also fun.

1. Take a first-semester physical education class. Most colleges require some type of physical education class to graduate. To get yourself started on a workout routine right away, simply schedule that class in your first semester. Consider ballroom dancing, tennis, swimming, or racquetball. For some courses, you will have to attend every day. Even on light days you will still be moving large muscle groups. Also, by having exercise scheduled into your day, you will establish a daily routine of keeping fit.

2. Participate in intramural sports. Intramural athletics are not only a great way to stay in shape, they're a wonderful way to make friends, especially for first-year students. The best thing about intramurals is that most of the time they are not seriously competitive. This enables everyone to participate. For those who do take winning and losing seriously, there are always a few teams that go all-out for intramurals. But for the vast majority of students, friendly competition and companionship are more than enough. You don't have to be great at the sport to participate. Fred was quite possibly the worst basketball player in the history of his high school, and he still shot hoops with college friends during freshman year. Fred reports that he and his friends would laugh about their skills (or rather, lack of skills), but it was an experience that burned calories and brought the group closer.

3. Say yes immediately to anything that keeps you moving. Spontaneous activity is sometimes the most enjoyable kind. College life is sedentary by nature. Lots of books, not enough outdoors. You must make moving a ritual and routine. Keep a Frisbee or small football in your bag at all times for those ten minutes between classes when you're bored and don't have anything else to do. You may not sweat, but it's a way to burn calories and speed up your heart rate. Spontaneous activity surprises your body in a good way. Researchers at the Mayo Clinic have studied the impact of everyday movements like pacing, fidgeting, and restlessness on body size. In their study, they found that overweight people sat for 150 minutes more per day on average than those who were lean. This difference translated into 350 fewer calories burned each day. They determined that if the overweight subjects matched the movement of their lean counterparts, they could lose thirty pounds a year (Chakravarthy, Joyner, and Booth 2002). So go ahead. Pace, fidget, or stretch your arms. Just don't sit still.

4. Take the long road. If you have any bit of extra time, whether it is between classes or jobs, take the longer route to your activities. If you have a class all the way across campus and you have an extra ten minutes, choose the longest distance to your destination. When you're in a building with both stairs and an elevator, take the steps. It sounds like a ridiculous idea, especially when you already feel tired, but it is spontaneous activity to boost your alertness and burn the apple fritter you may have had for breakfast. And seriously consider a pedometer.

Pete, a biology major planning to go to med school, tested strategy number 4: *Okay, this has definitely been easy to do. I walk the long way, even when it is below zero outside. I find myself looking for more inconvenient approaches, or what I call the "long cuts" rather than the shortcuts. These long cuts have been the cure for my laziness and tiredness and it seems to wake me up in the morning and make me alert for whatever I have on my to-do list. If I am pressed for time, I will revert to the shortcuts, but even then I refuse to use the elevator to go up or down just three flights of stairs. It has even been a factor in my social life. This past weekend I was invited to a friend's house off campus. Without even considering the idea of driving, I took out my walking boots. These changes in my routine seem to make my life less lazy and more proactive.*

Maybe buy two—one for you and one for your roommate—and keep track of who can take more steps in a week. The Centers for Disease Control actually recommends that people walk ten thousand steps a day, or about five miles. But that is a long way from the current reality. For instance, even in Colorado, the nation's leanest state, the average person walks fewer than three thousand steps a day (Hill 2003). But figure it this way: if you increase your steps by two thousand a day, you will burn 100 extra calories, which equals one pound of additional weight loss in a month.

5. Find a partner. Find someone with the same activity interests, whether it is lifting weights, running a few miles, or even playing hacky-sack. Once you've found that person, make an effort to spend time together. This is not just another way to make friends, it also helps keep both of you accountable. By having a partner who is as dedicated to fitness as you are, you'll be more likely to go work out—even when you feel like a slug inside.

6. Select an active work-study or job. You'll most likely be working some sort of job to help pay for college. Try to select a job that will require you to move.

Sitting behind a desk at the information center is a great way to catch up on homework, but it isn't going to burn fat. The solution? Find a job where movement is required. You can work as a custodian, on the grounds crew, or even as a cafeteria worker pushing trays and dishes around. Some colleges need attendants in the fitness center. These jobs aren't as easy as sitting behind a desk waiting for a phone to ring, but while you are working, you'll make friends and burn calories.

7. Select an active date. When thinking about what to do on a date, recommend something original and active. Let's face it— anyone can plan dinner and a movie. To be creative, think of something off the beaten path . . . literally! Find a trail for hiking or biking, or even take a long walk to a local historical or scenic site. This will serve two purposes: not only will you get to know the community, you will also get moving to burn off the day's fuel. After all, who doesn't want to look and feel fit on a date? A walk in the woods or a stroll in the park won't cost you any money, and that is always a plus. And wouldn't you rather date someone who is creative, interesting, and fit? This is a win-win situation!

8. Stretch in class. I'm sure anyone reading this book has become stiff, bored, or just plain uncomfortable sitting in a class. When your muscles get too stiff or remain in an uncomfortable position for a long period of time, you start to develop cramps and pain. These will only get worse (particularly in the neck, shoulders, and back) as you get older if you do nothing to address them. Now, putting your feet up on your desk is a great way to stretch out your legs, but it won't impress the professor. However, you can stretch in a discreet way when your teacher reaches a natural break in the lesson. Here are some quick stretches as recommended by Carolyn Hoffmann, LPT, the physical therapist you met in earlier in chapter 4.

- *Half shrug.* Sit upright. Bring your shoulders straight up to your ears, roll them back and down, then relax. Repeat this slowly. This helps relax your shoulders.

- *Turtle stretch.* Sit upright and move your head straight back while keeping your chin level. Repeat this slowly. This stretches the chin and neck.

- *Lower back.* Place your hand on the small of your back, then arch your back forward and back to ease the pressure from your lower back.

- *Stretch break.* If your professor gives you a stretch break, stand up and take advantage of the opportunity to improve your blood flow. Grab the top of your foot and bring your heel back to touch your hip. Do this with both legs. For your upper body, reach both arms out as far as they will stretch. Then reach toward your left hand with your right hand, like you were going to pull a long-sleeved sweater off.

9. **Dorm room workouts.** On days with no time to make it to the gym or pool, exercise in your dorm room. To work out in your dorm, you will need open floor space and a free wall. It also helps to have an understanding roommate who will appreciate your antics, or even support them by working out with you. With floor space, your roommate's blessing, and a comfortable outfit—you can get started. This workout won't give you arms like Popeye, or legs like a track star, but when practiced daily for a period of three weeks, they will shape and tone your abs, chest, and back. Here is a simple routine for a Dorm Room Workout, as recommended by Carolyn Hoffmann, LPT.

- *Wall push-ups.* Even in a small dorm room with little free wall space, you will be able to stand and face a closed door. Put your arms out and lean in toward the door. With your feet shoulder-width apart, push yourself back and forth against the door. Repeat this five to ten times.

- *Side bender.* With your arms at your side, bring your right arm up over your head and gently lean toward your left side while also reaching toward the floor with your left hand. Repeat this five to ten times, then switch sides.

- *Calf muscle stretch.* Place one foot ahead of the other. With the back heel flat on the floor, lean in toward the front foot. Repeat this five to ten times with each leg.

- *Traditional crunch.* Lie on your back and bend your knees so your feet rest on the floor. With arms stretched out to the front, lift shoulders off the floor about forty-five degrees. Slowly lower shoulders back to the floor. Repeat five to ten times.

- *Traditional push-up.* Lie face down on the floor. Place hands next to your shoulders, fingers pointing straight ahead. Place feet a few inches apart, toes on floor. Tightening abs, extend elbows to raise body off floor. Keeping head aligned with

Pete tested strategy number 9: *I tried to work out right away in the morning before showering and at night before bed, and in the midafternoon between classes. I have found it most effective between classes at three in the afternoon. After my school day had ended and before my evening had began, this revved me up for the next chunk of the day so I didn't fall off into a soft decline. It refreshes me and is easy to do anywhere. On weekends, I do this workout while watching TV, listening to music, or watching a movie.*

spine, lower your body four to eight inches from floor. Repeat five to ten times.

- *Swimming.* Lying face down, extend your arms in front of you and your legs behind you. Keeping arms and legs straight, lift the right arm and left leg off the floor. As they lower down, lift the left arm and right leg so it looks like you are swimming. Repeat five to ten times. This works the often-neglected lower back muscles.

10. Fad workouts from late-night TV. The early 1990s cemented the fad workout in our lives. From circuit training to Tae Bo and spinning, we have flocked and bought into the allure. These programs meet our simple need for structure and consistency. Many of these exercise and weight-loss programs are effective, so if you love to follow the popular culture of fitness, go ahead and try the latest late-night TV fad workout. With your roommate's blessing, a VCR or a DVD player, and enough floor space in your dorm room, you can work out on your own schedule.

11. Study yoga. Yoga is appealing because the lifestyle is synonymous with relaxation and less stress. People who practice yoga say it is a way to connect to inner energy and release full physical potential. It's pretty easy to get started. Borrow a book or a videotape from the library or join a class on campus. Yoga improves your core muscles, flexibility, coordination, balance, and self-confidence. Here's how:

- *Increased flexibility.* When you practice a variety of yoga positions, your body is stretched in different ways than in other workouts.
- *Increased lubrication of the joints, ligaments, and tendons.* Reaching the top shelf of your closet or carrying laundry up the steps will also be easier with yoga in your schedule.

- *Massaging of all organs in the body.* During a yoga session, your internal organs and glands are stimulated. Yoga is a way to specifically increase blood flow to internal organs, which helps keep your body disease free and provides more sensitive feelings of changes in how your body feels. With the increased blood flow, yoga may be a way to flush out toxins from your system. The ultimate benefit is feeling like you have more energy.

- *Muscle toning.* When a muscle sits dormant for a period of time, it will become weak and flabby. Since yoga is a full-body workout, your weakest muscles will get stronger.

12. Practice Pilates. Like Yoga, Pilates is a workout that emphasizes core body movement without weight and relies on your own muscles to build power and flexibility. This method of exercise is widely popular with dancers and skaters. While yoga promotes calmness and flexibility, Pilates is more focused on building strength through motion. Joseph Pilates, who overcame a frail body as a child to eventually become an accomplished skier, gymnast, and boxer, developed this

Christa, an elementary ed major from Iowa, tested strategy number 12: *I have enjoyed the Winsor Pilates workout tape every night before I go to bed. It has been good for stretching and is an easy routine to get into. I think that either doing this in the morning or at night before bed is something simple than anyone can do. It leaves you feeling better about yourself. I have found it to be stress relieving and a good way to go to sleep.*

method. While yoga is a full-body workout, Pilates works core muscles—the chest, abs, and all the muscles connected to your back. You might say to yourself, "I do crunches every night . . . isn't that enough?" Well, yes and no. Pilates works muscles missed with crunches. With a stronger core, your balance and coordination will improve. These traits will be noticeable even in walking. A good way to describe what Pilates does is that it supports your body in the same way that a tree supports its branches. A tree can't support all its branches if its trunk isn't strong. In other words, if you work your arms, shoulders, and legs through traditional exercise, you should also give your trunk strength to support them through Pilates. It is especially helpful for anyone who has experienced back pain.

13. Find a new hobby or rediscover an old one. Keeping fit is easier if your thoughts of chilling out travel farther than the nearest snack machine. Students we surveyed said they developed new hobbies when they got to college or they even resumed hobbies they had as children. Here are a few examples:

- Scrapbooking
- Beading
- Painting or drawing
- Playing the guitar or piano
- Writing songs
- Composing poetry
- Keeping a diary

All of these hobbies, while sedentary, exercise your mind and keep your hands out of the candy machine.

14. Keep your room clean. Let's face it, if you aren't motivated enough to pick up a few dirty socks, how on earth are you going to be able to motivate yourself to lift weights or take the longer road to class? With clothes all over the floor, books and magazines in every corner, and a bed that hasn't been made since moving day, you are going to feel disorganized and unmotivated. Keeping your room clean will give you a fresh, organized feeling every time you walk into it, which will give you more energy for the other activities you do. Being active about keeping your room picked up is another way to combat the freshman fifteen.

15. Volunteer on campus. Whether you're interested in hunger relief, animal rights, or science fiction literature, there is probably a club that is right for you. Such clubs usually include taking on some responsibility, from attending meetings to working at fund-raisers. Staying active and involved with others keeps you from mindless eating, so volunteer and become a responsible member. If you're really into taking photos, then join the photography club. Or join a group to learn something totally new. It might be a human rights organization or a first amendment advocacy group, but you'll never fully understand your passions and interests unless you experiment with new experiences and relationships. And while you are thinking about new things, you won't be eating.

STICK WITH IT

Every journey begins with a first step. By reading this book, you have taken the first step toward improving your fitness and your life. Remember, this is your ride, your body, your life. You are the only one who can make the change. The most difficult period will be the first two days. Then try this: For three weeks, just twenty-one days, accept the fact that you'll be in uncharted territory. It takes twenty-one days to cement a new habit. Once you have committed yourself to change, you will start to see that exercise is a gift you have given yourself. You do have control over how you look and feel. It is not just your body that feels stronger. There is something inside of you that gets stronger too.

DOCUMENT YOUR NEW, ACTIVE LIFESTYLE

College years are a time to remember. You're experiencing so many new things that time seems to fly by, and your first year will be gone before you know it. To remember all your great times and the emergence of a new lifestyle, think of a way to record what you've experienced over the year. This can be as easy as writing in a journal, taking photos with all your friends, or creating a scrapbook chock-full of mementos, like concert tickets or a program from an art show. As time goes by, you'll appreciate that you made an effort to remember what you experienced. But, there's an important key to having things to remember—you have to actually go out and try activities so that you actually have things to remember.

Signs of Exercise Abuse

Zealous attitudes about exercise can be taken to dangerous levels, and health professionals now recognize this problem as exercise abuse (Jackson 2005). It may occur along with disordered eating. Be aware of signs like these that suggest a compulsion with physical activity:

- A strong emotional commitment to exercise that disrupts relationships
- A sense of obligation to exercise, evidenced by an inability to take a day off
- Anxiety when exercise is not possible

- A rigid relationship between eating and output—having to exercise after eating
- Lack of enjoyment of the exercise activity
- Exercise during illness or injury
- Exercise at the expense of other responsibilities
- Continuous talking about exercise
- Exercise in secret
- A preoccupation with exercise supplements or products leading to financial hardship

The point is to be aware that even healthy habits can be taken to extremes. Maintaining fitness and preventing weight gain are not impossible goals for your freshman year. They can be achieved through educated decisions about eating and an active lifestyle. But don't focus on being perfect. Everyone has off days, and you will too. Making good choices as often as you can and aiming for "most of the time" will help you feel better about yourself. So why not start right now?

sleep: why what happens at night can mean everything to your day

After a long day of classes, the late shift at work, or just experiencing the mayhem of your dorm hallway, you retreat to the quiet sanctuary of your room. As you climb into your bed, wrap yourself in the sheets and attempt to fall asleep, you suddenly remember that you have a biology quiz tomorrow and you haven't opened the book yet. As you climb out of bed, you tell yourself, "Missing an hour of sleep won't kill me," and you study longer. You nail the quiz and feel fine. But as those nights of short sleep become the norm rather than an occasional thing, you begin to see the effects. You begin to feel drained and tired all day.

Of course, there will be nights when you will sleep less, whether it is after a big concert or when you're studying for finals. But chronic sleep loss adds up to being more than tired and grouchy. Lost sleep can cause problems like these:

- Inability to focus in class
- Increased likelihood of weight gain
- Impaired immunity to viruses and common illnesses
- Diminished creativity
- Forgetfulness and being prone to accidents

When asked to rank a list of wellness concerns, students we interviewed identified sleep problems as second in importance of what they were concerned about. This chapter will reveal the science behind good sleep and the relationship between sleep and daily vitality. It will convince you once and for all that sleep matters more than you thought. In this chapter, you will also learn about these issues:

- Why naps are not just for preschoolers
- How caffeine affects sleep
- Which bedtime snacks help you snooze
- Why you can't just catch up on weekends

what students said:

I got a cold and ended up taking Nyquil for nearly a month to get to sleep.

I would like to get eight hours, but that is not realistic. I learned to take naps—quick ones.

Sleep problems led to fatigue and affected my studies. I could function well on five hours during the week, then slept about nine hours a night on weekends.

My sleep habits were bad! *I was happy to get in bed by 2 A.M. any day of the week. Many all-nighters.*

Normally I need eight hours of sleep a night, but I adjusted to about five or six—I felt deprived.

First, a definition. "Sleep: the natural periodic suspension of consciousness during which the powers of the body are restored" (Merriam-Webster 2003).

"Natural periodic suspension of consciousness" refers to the fact that when you're sleeping, you aren't doing any of your other daily tasks, such as thinking, reading, learning, working, or socializing. It also means that sleep is not the same as rest. Rest can mean watching TV, reading a magazine, or talking on the telephone. Rest is important, but it is sleep that is directly related to productivity.

Sleep is a period in which, as the definition says, "the powers of the body are restored." Those restorative powers aren't limited to the physical act of getting up, turning off the alarm and starting the day, but also to your ability to process thoughts in your morning class. Without proper rest and regeneration at night, you're only going to be operating at half your cognitive potential.

Here is a metaphor about sleep and college: Think about your cellular phone. When your phone goes completely dead, what do you do? You charge it all the way back to full power, because, as most students know, if you only charge it partway each time, you'll eventually wear the battery down to nothing. Okay, now your mind is the battery. If you're only charging your mind a little bit at a time, over and over, rather than letting it return to full strength, your mind power will eventually be diminished. Get the picture?

Sleep Science

Sleep is even more important to college students than for older adults. Young adults are naturally more active. After all, when was the last time you saw your grandmother pull an all-nighter and then make it to a concert the next night? Sleep scientists say students age eighteen to twenty-four need between seven and a half and nine hours of sleep a night to perform at their best level (Kindler 2004). Unfortunately, as we found in student interviews, most college students fail to achieve proper rest.

Over 80 percent of the students we surveyed believed they were seriously sleep deprived. On average, these students were sleeping six hours a night. The least amount of sleep reported was an average of five hours, and the most for any student was a consistent nine hours a night.

So, if you are anything like an average student, over the course of one week, that means you are losing ten to fifteen hours of sleep. Those hours you missed are comparable to giving up a whole night of sleep one day a week, every week of the school year.

LESS SLEEP EQUALS MORE WEIGHT

Can sleep deficits make you fat? Think about it, college students. It is very common to experience both sleep disruptions and weight gain in college. The science is just starting to catch up with this observation.

Behavioral scientists have found that sleep deprivation increases levels of a hunger hormone and decreases levels of a satiety hormone (Spiegel et al. 2004). These sleep-related hormonal fluctuations lead to overeating and weight gain, a pattern experienced by many college students.

At the University of Chicago, sleep researcher Eve Van Cauter has been studying this phenomenon for twenty-five years. Dr. Cauter says sleep deprivation activates a small part of the hypothalamus (Spiegel et al. 2004). This is the region of the brain that produces the hormones central to appetite control. These hormones, known as *ghrelin* and *leptin*, impact our eating behavior in different ways. Ghrelin is released by cells in the stomach and stimulates the appetite. It is the body chemical that gives us a hungry feeling. The other hormone, leptin, is released by our fat cells and tells our brain that we are full. When leptin is working right, our brains get the message that we have eaten.

In one of her studies, Dr. Cauter invited twelve healthy and normal-weight young men to sleep and eat dinner and breakfast in her laboratory. The average age of her participants was twenty-two years old. For two consecutive nights, study participants were limited to four hours of sleep. For another two consecutive nights, participants were permitted ten hours of sleep. At the end of the short and long sleep periods, blood tests showed that leptin levels were 18 percent lower and ghrelin levels were 28 percent higher in study subjects after the four-hour sleep period. The sleep-deprived subjects with the biggest hormonal changes also reported feeling the most hungry. They craved cake, candy, ice cream, pasta, and bread. Those who had the smallest hormonal changes reported being the least hungry (Spiegel et al. 2004). One of the subjects was a DePaul University biology major. He said that after getting only four hours of sleep for two straight nights, he was so hungry, he could have eaten his pillow.

Why is sleep so important to appetite control? The body's hormones have a twenty-four-hour rhythm, says Joyce Walsleben, Ph.D., the director of the Sleep Disorder Center at the New York University School of Medicine. When sleep is disrupted, hormones fall out of their rhythm and appetite may be stimulated due to changes in glucose metabolism (Sorgen 2003). This problem can lead not only to weight gain, but also to an increased risk of developing diabetes later in life.

The topic has garnered the interest of scientists across the country, from Stanford University to the University of Chicago. The idea is that when we are sleep deprived, hormonal control of metabolism is disrupted. Other studies have also shown a relationship between sleep deprivation, hormones, and weight. The Wisconsin Sleep Cohort Study, which tracked over a thousand people, found that people who slept five hours a night had higher ghrelin and lower leptin levels than those who slept eight hours (Taheri et al. 2004).

Researchers at Columbia University also found that people who slept two to four hours a night were 73 percent more likely to be obese than those who got seven to nine hours. This relationship played out in a predictable and alarming pattern for college students. Those who experienced five hours of sleep a night were 50 percent more likely to be obese, and those who slept six hours were 23 percent more likely to be obese than students who got more sleep (NAASO 2004).

In a way, all of these studies appear counterintuitive. You'd think that sleeping too much would contribute to making people fat. But the opposite is true. Sleep-deprived people eat more because they are truly hungry. They are awake longer and tempted by foods during all wakeful hours. They simply consume more calories than they burn in the extra hours they're awake.

NYU's Dr. Walsleben goes so far as to warn, "When we're young, we think we can get by on little—or even no—sleep at all. That's just not true. We all have to plan our life around getting enough sleep" (Sorgen 2003).

SLEEP FOSTERS CREATIVITY & PROBLEM SOLVING

Recently, German scientists confirmed what creative minds have known all along: our sleeping brains continue working on problems that baffle us during the day, and the right answer comes more easily after eight hours of rest (Associated Press 2004). The German findings are the first hard evidence supporting the idea that creativity and problem solving are linked to adequate sleep. In this study, doctors at the University of Luebeck found that volunteers who had eight hours of sleep and took a simple math test were three times more likely than sleep-deprived participants to figure out a hidden rule for finding correct answers. Jan Born, who directed the testing, said the results support biochemical studies that indicate our memories are restructured before they are stored as sharpened thoughts. Creativity also appears to be enhanced in the process. It appears that memories start deep in the brain, in the hippocampus, and are eventually pushed outward to the neocortex. The German study is expert proof that if you are serious about succeeding in college, you need to respect your need for sleep.

THE BEST KINDS OF SLEEP: REM & NREM

There are two types of sleep: rapid eye movement (REM) and nonrapid eye movement (NREM). While you are falling asleep, you are in NREM sleep. There are four stages of NREM sleep. The latter stages, three and four are termed *delta sleep*, and these stages are the most restful. Following these stages, REM sleep takes over. It is a period of increased brain activity. In this essential phase of sleep, you dream and your breathing and heart rate speed up.

A healthy sleep pattern is one in which you experience plenty of the NREM delta sleep followed by REM sleep. During these times, your body is at its deepest rest.

WHAT ABOUT DREAMS

Most dreaming occurs during REM sleep. In college, the common nightmare is waking up late to find out you forgot to turn in a final paper for a required class and will fail to graduate on time. You arouse from the fitful image, sit up straight in bed, look at the clock and say, "Thank God. It was only a bad dream!"

Scientists have great interest in the psychology of dreams. There are countless incidental and some famous reports of people solving great problems by "sleeping on it." The REM period of sleep is the time when the brain goes to work on issues of the day. It is as if the brain juggles old information into new and sensible patterns when we sleep. Eric Nofzinger, director of the sleep Neuroimaging Program at the University of Pittsburgh Medical Center, studies brain activity and thinks that could be why people often figure out thorny problems in their dreams (Kantrowitz 2004).

The bottom line is that you have to get enough sleep so that you have time to dream. If you want to make use of your dreams, try to extend the REM phase by remaining quiet and repeating the scenes from the dream until they become a firm memory. Or you may keep a journal by your bed and write down the details of the dream as soon as you wake up.

While there is lots of argument about the real meaning of dreams, scientists theorize that dreaming may help prepare us for potential disasters. For example, when college students dream they have forgotten to show up for a final test, the dream is a rehearsal for dealing with a real fear. Dreaming can also help you find solutions to elusive problems. Focusing on a dilemma before falling to sleep might be a way to kick-start a powerful and revealing REM dream.

SLEEPLESS NIGHTS EQUAL IRRITABLE DAYS

Nearly all students experience stress as a normal part of the college experience, and insomnia only makes things worse. When worries wake us in the middle of a REM cycle, issues that might have been resolved through dreams are left up in the air. Dreams tend to get more positive as sleep continues, and waking up too soon cuts this cycle short. It makes sense that people who are sleep deprived are cranky. They have not worked through the nasty feelings of the day. Get this: Rats eventually die when they don't get any REM sleep. The good news is that humans can keep going for a while even on four-hour sleep nights. Yet there is a true human need to sleep deeply enough to dream. In fact, when deprived of quality sleep, humans begin to have vivid dreams during their waking hours. You cannot save up sleep or REM time during weekend sleep-a-thons. You need at least seven hours of sleep every night. Establishing a regular bedtime and sticking to it is the best way to find the best quality sleep, ensure that your creative potential is met, and realize the benefit of problem-solving dreams.

Sleep tip: To maximize dreams for purposes of problem solving and creativity, go to bed and get up at a regular time every day (weekends included), stay away from caffeine and alcohol before bed, develop sleep rituals, and avoid bright lights in the bedroom. Good sleep produces good dreams and you will study better, feel smarter, and be more creative the next day.

Problems Related to Sleep Deprivation

More than seventy million Americans are sleep deprived, which is contributing to increased accidents, worsening overall health, and (in the case of students) lower test scores (Twersky 2000). "Most college students

. . . have 'social insomnia,'" says Dale Steffens, supervisor of the sleeping disorders unit at Iowa Lutheran Hospital. "They party or put off studying . . . and build up a sleep debt which eventually has to be repaid" (Pfeiffer 1997). In other words, most college students know they need sleep but put it off to go out drinking or hang out with their friends.

The body's immune system, as you'll remember from biology class, features the T cells and phagocytes that kick viruses and infectious agents out of your cells. It turns out they are literally not on the job if you are chronically sleep deprived. Immune cells need proteins that are regenerated with a healthy diet and plenty of sleep. If you are catching every little sniffle that comes along, lack of sleep probably has something to do with it.

It's also difficult to control your emotions when you're tired. Minor frustrations can feel so heavy when you are without sleep. Because fatigue causes impulsiveness and poor focus, symptoms of fatigue can appear to be similar to attention-deficit/hyperactivity disorder. Loss of sleep also slows reaction time. Slow reaction times can result in automobile accidents: every year, drowsy driving results in 56,000 automobile accidents and 1,550 fatalities; almost two-thirds of these crashes are caused by drivers under age thirty (Mayo Clinic Staff 2005a). When you place an emphasis on sleep and proper rest during the day, your body is much more likely to perform at the level it is capable of.

Alcohol disrupts the sleep center of the brain. Though a few beers may give you a relaxed feeling, booze actually interrupts the natural sleep cycle. If someone snoozes while under the influence of booze, don't assume he or she will experience the restorative power of rest. Sleeping while inebriated results in moodiness, irritability, and hangovers. Hangovers are all about being tired and dehydrated. Hangovers are actually depression of the central nervous system and constriction of the circulatory vessels. This is why sleep, aspirin, and fluids are the remedy for hangover symptoms.

Here are some signs that you may not be getting enough sleep:

- You routinely sleep through your alarm clock.
- You think about sleep and catching up on the weekends.
- You have to fight to stay awake during class.
- You are easily agitated with friends and family.
- You have difficulty concentrating or remembering details.
- You wake up repeatedly through the night.
- You feel groggy more than half of the day .

Snacks, Exercise, & Bedtime Rituals

Did you know that sugars and fats in bedtime snacks influence the way you sleep? Eating a stack of cookies before bed might make you sleepy, but after a few hours, it will wear off. This is because your blood sugar falls, which makes you hungry again even though you may have eaten a few hours prior. We know what you're thinking, "I've gone to bed hungry a lot of times before." If you've fallen asleep, you weren't really hungry. When you are hungry, your body will remain alert until you feed it. The easiest way to avoid either one of these problems is to eat something healthy.

Sleep tip: The best snacks are usually low in sugar and fat, such as nonsweetened cereals and skim milk, or wheat crackers and string cheese or yogurt. These choices will fill you up so you can relax; they will also keep your blood sugar at a constant level throughout the night. Sound sleep will result.

EXERCISE ALSO AFFECTS SLEEP

A good workout will invigorate your body, help you fall asleep faster, and help you sleep longer than if you don't exercise at all. Exercise may overstimulate some people, so it is best done several hours before bedtime. By now, most of you have probably figured out that when you exercise, you feel good about yourself. Those "feel good" emotions are produced by body chemicals called *endorphins*. Endorphins help you deal with daily stresses, which in turn will help you become less stressed as bedtime approaches. The end result? With less anxiety, you will fall asleep and experience solid rest for long periods of time.

OUT LIKE A LIGHT

Okay, so we've convinced you about the importance of sleep. Here are some practical tips for hitting the pillow and conking out. And even it if it's not realistic for you to get eight to nine hours of sleep a night, these tips will help you maximize your rest or train yourself to function better on less sleep.

- *Create a bedtime routine.* This signals your brain that sleep is on the way. If that means having a few Oreos and a glass of milk, brushing your teeth, and then showering before bed, great!
- *Drink water, and lots of it.* To sleep well, your body must be hydrated properly. Drink eight to ten cups per day, and drink more when you are physically active.
- *Seek absolute peacefulness.* When you do sleep, make it count. Make sure your room is always perfectly quiet, very dark, and well ventilated. Open a window, even if only a crack, for fresh air.

Brandon, a music major: *It is becoming easier to go to bed at the same time and get up at the same time in the morning. The more I do this, the easier it gets. Also, slipping in naps in the afternoon for a little extra energy is helping and is very refreshing for a second wind for the rest of the day. It seems that I am less tired during the day the more regular my sleep pattern gets. With keeping a steady bedtime, I ensure that I get at least seven and a half hours of sleep each night. I have also tried to drink less caffeine and more water. Getting regular sleep has helped me feel better throughout the day.*

Brad, a journalism major who works long hours: *I am one that in the past has completely ignored the importance of sleep. Since my freshman year, I have gone to bed, on the average, at three in the morning and I have*

- *Move large muscle groups.* If you're so busy you don't have enough time to sleep, an hour workout at the gym might not be an option, but even light exercise can help make the sleep you do get more meaningful. Take the long way home, say a brisk twenty-minute walk, from your last class of the day. Remember, exercise produces endorphins and helps you sleep at an optimized level even if your personal schedule dictates a shorter sleep.

- *Take a hot shower.* Scrubbing yourself from head to toe is always refreshing and relaxing, and it can become a signal for the end of your day. If you have a bathtub, a hot bath can also be very soothing.

- *Make your room a sleep haven.* This will have to be done in conjunction with your roommate's wishes, but make your room the ultimate place to sleep. If that means having total darkness and silence, that can be accomplished by putting curtains around your bed to block out all light. Silence comes with earplugs. If you need music to fall asleep but your roommate needs silence, then buy inner ear headphones. You will get your tunes without disturbing your roommate.

- *Read a book or magazine.* That doesn't mean a textbook or a journal article for a class. It means a good novel or the latest copy of *Rolling Stone*. Reading will relax your mind and tire your eye muscles, signaling them to rest.
- *Make your bed every day.* A bed made with the sheets and blankets tucked in tightly and wrinkles all smoothed out invites sleep. Oh, and wash the sheets at least once a month. It's amazing what clean linens do for sleep.

SLEEP SOFTWARE

What if you are ready to sleep and climb into your bed . . . but still find problems? Maybe the bed is too soft, or it's hard as a brick. Try these tips:

- *Make it like it was at home.* Think about your bed back home—it probably always seemed warm, inviting, and perfect, just what you were used to. To sleep well, simply re-create that bed at college. Modify the mattress. Most dorm mattresses are relatively neutral—not quite rocks, but not waterbeds either. You can easily

pulled about fifteen all-nighters. With this in mind, I started going to sleep at a regular time and I am pretty impressed by the results. Now, instead of hitting the snooze button about ten times because I am so tired, I actually feel ready for the day. I seem to be able to concentrate more in class. Spending a month practicing nothing but going to bed early is amazing. I cannot imagine how I made it with no sleep before. I used to wake up feeling drained. Taking a shower when I woke up used to be the only thing I could do to fully wake up. Now, waking up with a full night's rest feels so good and so different. Class goes so much better. I don't feel sleepy during the day and I am much more attentive. It is so wonderful.

adjust how you want the mattress to feel. If you like a firm-feeling mattress without much give, simply place boards between the box springs and the mattress. This will create a firmer feel. If you prefer a softer mattress, buy some bubbletop bed foam from any department store. The foam can go under the mattress to create lift, but it's best to place it directly under the mattress cover and sleep directly on top of it. This will give you the pillow-top feel of newer mattresses. If you're a poor college student, Egyptian cotton, satin, or silk sheets will probably be out of your budget, but invest in the best cotton sheets you can afford. The thread count on the package is an indication of quality. Aim for 128-count cotton. Some students use the sheets they had on their bed at home. If you have new sheets, washing them a few times will help soften them up.

- *Examine your pillows—the most important software of sleep.* If you are used to a feather pillow, bring it from home. Be sure to get a pillow that supports your neck at a comfortable angle— not too high or too low. It should help position your neck on a relatively even plane with your body. If your pillow doesn't fit these characteristics, it can cause neck and shoulder pain. For another version of true comfort, buy a body pillow and sleep with one end under your head and the other between your legs. This will keep your spine aligned, which will cut down on backaches. Don't be afraid to have lots of pillows. Surround your bed on all sides, and your bed will double as a couch.

SLEEP HARDWARE

Now that we've taken care of your mattress, what about the bed itself?

Lofts are wonderful for college students. They conserve space, provide more room to move, and generally look pretty cool. After all, who doesn't want the top bunk? But when creating a loft, ask yourself, "How high do I want to be when I stumble out of bed in the morning?" After all, it is easy to climb up before you fall asleep, but when you're waking up early for class, climbing down can be more difficult. So if you do decide a loft is what you want, invest in a nice ladder or build one into the frame of the loft itself. It will save you a lot of unnecessary foot and ankle pain in the mornings.

No one likes looking at blank walls. Buy posters of your favorite bands or models and put them up around your bed. It will make your room feel more like home. Hang pictures from home, such as photos of old friends, grandparents, or your brothers and sisters. Or print out inspirational quotes from your favorite poets or musicians and post those on the back of the door.

Napping

Almost everyone hated nap time in kindergarten. It just got in the way of recess. However, in college napping can be a savior; and for some students, it's part of their daily routine. Over half of the students we surveyed said that they made napping a priority during the day, and every student said that naps were beneficial to them at some point during the year.

Napping can either enhance or disrupt a sleep pattern. If you have trouble falling asleep at night, daytime napping is probably not the best idea since it may increase insomnia. But if, like most students, you have trouble meeting your daily sleep requirements, taking a regular nap may be the answer. Napping is a part of the regular routine in other cultures. Persons of some Spanish and Latin American cultures nap between one and four o'clock in the afternoon. In these cultures, people recognize that the human body is inclined to rest, or drop off in energy, in the afternoon as well as at night. This comes from a slight drop in body temperature and alertness that occurs in the afternoon. This effect is smaller, but very similar, to what happens to your body when you fall asleep at night. By taking an afternoon nap, you can reenergize yourself for the rest of the day without affecting the sleep you experience at night.

Napping should be limited to twenty to thirty minutes. This amount may not seem long, but it can be enough to restore energy to enjoy the evening. If you sleep longer than thirty minutes, you will enter a deep sleep, which will only make it difficult for you to wake up. It's helpful to set an alarm for thirty minutes. You can relax, sleep for a short time, and know that you are going to wake up with the alarm. However, if your lack of sleep is so great that you need a longer nap, sleep for at least ninety minutes. This will enable you to complete a sleep cycle, which will bring you even more rest.

Sleep tip: Plan your naps. Put thirty minutes of shut-eye into your daily planner. If you arrive at that time you designated and aren't tired, use the block of time to relax by reading a book, watching television, or lying down with your eyes closed. This rest will enable you to keep saving stored energy while keeping your sleep pattern intact. If there is a time when you know you will be up late and get less sleep than you normally do, be proactive. Take a nap ahead of time, banking a portion of your sleep. Seriously planning for your sleep needs makes it more likely you'll perform well on your tasks the next day.

Negotiating Sleep Issues with Your Roommate

Although it sounds simple to get along with a roommate and respect each other's sleep according to each other's needs, it is hardly ever the case. Roommates are usually selected to be somewhat compatible with each other, but you may find out that in some ways you lead very different lives and have different schedules. These differences can drastically change the way you sleep. To sleep well, you and your roommate will have to communicate with each other. Here are five helpful questions to ask.

1. **What time will you go to bed?** Sounds simple, but this is a difficult question. If you go to bed early every night for an eight o'clock class and your roommate likes to stay up late playing computer games, you will have a problem. From the first night, make it very clear what time you want to go to bed every night, and then stick to it. If the situation is reversed and your roommate is an early-to-bed person while you're a night owl, be sympathetic to the quiet your roommate needs. The easiest thing to do is to find a common time when both of you can agree to either get ready for bed or be whisper-quiet.

2. **How do you usually fall asleep: with music or TV or having the room quiet?** Some people like to fall asleep watching late-night talk shows or listening to music, while others must fall asleep in complete silence. With those kinds of differences, one of you may be struggling to get to sleep.

3. **What room atmosphere do you prefer?** Room atmosphere has everything to do with how you sleep. Some people sleep very well in a warm room with few blankets. Others like a very cool

room with a consistent breeze or a fan blowing. It is important to find a middle ground. If one of you likes a warm room and the other needs an icebox, separate the beds. The person who prefers heat can find it in the corner far away from the breeze. The other roommate can sleep next to an open window.

4. **Do you have any weird habits?** This question will be a hard one to ask your roommate, but if you don't, you could be in for a surprise during the night. One of the students we surveyed had a roommate who talked in her sleep. She also sleepwalked from time to time. Her roomate had no idea, since the sleepwalker never explained her habits. Imagine how surprised you would be to see the person you live with (and don't know very well yet) walking around and mumbling like a zombie? To avoid that situation, it's best to clear the air and discuss any habits like that immediately. As long as you and your roommate agree on the importance of sleep and know what you're expecting from each other, you both will meet your sleep needs.

5. **What time will you wake up?** This question depends on your agenda for the day, but it is good to know in advance. Over half of the students we surveyed said that their roommates were on different schedules than their own, which created differing sleeping times. It can be somewhat distracting to have a roommate who starts doing homework at 7:30 A.M. if you had been planning on sleeping in. The best solution is to pick a time to wake up every day and stick to it. If that time is different than your roommate's, then be courteous. If your roommate is still asleep when you wake up, do things quietly. Don't slam the door. Do your work in a study lounge area or the library until your roommate wakes up.

If sleep issues become a chronic conflict between you and your roommate, talking things out hasn't changed the situation, and you feel your academic and creative performance are suffering, then it's time to take action. Consider moving to a designated quiet or wellness floor and rooming with a person who values the same lifestyle.

Crunch Time & Caffeine

From a young age, we learn that caffeine can affect our behavior. We've all had nights when we are wired because of too much Mountain Dew or too many brownies.

How does caffeine work? Caffeine is a bitter-tasting chemical that is found in plants, including cocoa and coffee beans, as well as tea leaves. Caffeine can also be created artificially. Caffeine affects your body because it is similar in structure to the chemical adenosine, which slows down the central nervous system. When the two chemicals are present in the body, they compete for bonding sites in the nervous system. Adenosine activity is depressed, and as a result, you feel the high or energy that is most associated with caffeine.

While everyone is affected by caffeine intake, the degree of the effect is very individual. When given similar doses, some people might only experience a minimal jump in energy, while others feel totally hyped up. Whichever reaction you have depends on your natural tolerance for the drug. For example, hard-core coffee drinkers might not get much of a jump, if any, from one can of soda. But that same can, when given to a person who avoids caffeine, can cause jitters.

Caffeine is also a diuretic, meaning it dehydrates your body and leaves all your cells thirsty and weak. This means your body will need more sleep and lots of water to rejuvenate it. In reality, it defeats the purpose of drinking caffeine to perk up, doesn't it? Make no mistake, caffeine is both a diuretic and a drug, when used the wrong way. Many people, especially young adults and teenagers, can develop a caffeine addiction. Used in moderation and in concert with sleep cycles, however, caffeine is safe.

Sleep Disorders Common in College

Even with proper planning for sleep, there can be problems that deserve attention. Sleep disorders are common among young adults. Here are a few types:

1. **Obstructive sleep apnea.** Sleep apnea involves episodes of paused breathing during nighttime sleep that can occur up to several hundred times a night. Snoring is one warning sign of this.

2. **Narcolepsy.** This is a disorder characterized by excessive daytime sleepiness and periods of muscle weakness.

3. **Insomnia.** This is a very common sleep disorder that keeps you awake night after night and eventually leads to sleep deprivation. Insomnia has many forms and causes but, thankfully, just as many treatments.

4. **Sleepwalking.** This disorder goes hand in hand with talking in your sleep. Neither is harmful, although in the case of sleepwalking, you need to sleep in a room on a ground floor that is free of clutter and obstacles.

If you believe that you have a sleep disorder, you have many helpful options available to you. Sleep therapists can help diagnose and treat the problem, and your campus health services office should be able to refer you to the right setting for help.

Bottom Line: Sleep Impacts your Academic Performance

Nearly every college student will be challenged to meet his or her sleep needs. Living on campus is like staying in a motel, only you're going to be there for nine months and share the room with someone who might snore. It is a process of trial and error and finding out what works for you. Don't be shy about experimenting with a power nap. If you know you need to sleep in on Saturday, don't feel guilty. But make no mistake, chronic sleep deprivation eventually catches up with you. Expect weight gain, irritability, and loss of focus. If you started college with the vision of doing well, sleep has everything to do with performing at your academic best.

finding healthy releases for stress

Stress is a part of life at any age. When you're seven, you're wondering if you're going to get that new toy for Christmas. When you're seventeen, you're wondering how to ask that cute classmate out on a date. When you're twenty-seven, you're wondering if you're ever going to find someone to marry. When you're thirty-seven, you're probably scrambling to pay for a house and a car and save for your kid's college fund. When you're forty-seven, you're probably wondering what it would be like to be twenty-seven again . . . It is a vicious cycle. Thankfully, stress relief can be found in many out-of-the-way places, as well as in traditional comforts.

What the Science Says About Stress

Dr. Wayne Kelly, MD, a board-certified family physician, is the medical director at Student Health Services for Winona State University. He has cared for college students for twenty years. He explained stress to us in this way:

> Stress is anything that interferes with a person's mental or physical well-being. It impacts one's feelings of happiness or sadness and takes on different forms in different people.
>
> Some forms of stress that drastically affect one person might not bother another person at all. So stress is very subjective, depending upon the environment and priorities and interests of the individual at a particular moment in time. This is why people respond differently to stress during certain situations in their lives.
>
> Stress can affect people in many different ways. For some individuals, the symptoms might be an unexplainable body ache, often as neck, shoulder, or back pain. It can also be present in the form of headaches, upset stomach, nausea, or vomiting.

what students said:

My number one way to de-stress was listening to music.

I got stressed-out from trying to balance homework with sleep time.

My number one wellness concern was actually questioning my mental health. Could I handle the stress of college?

I needed other motivational techniques besides calling my mom.

Now, each of these symptoms can have an underlying physical cause. Therefore, a careful history and careful physical exam can help sort this out. As I talk to students about stress, I ask about their habits and lifestyle. (Kelly 2004)

Signs of Extreme Stress

Here are some physical, behavioral, mental, and emotional cues that stress has become a problem:

Physical cues. Fatigue, headache, insomnia, muscle aches/stiffness (especially in the neck, shoulders, and back), chest pains, abdominal cramps, nausea, trembling, cold extremities, sweats, frequent colds or flus, weight gain or loss.

Behavioral cues. Smoking, drinking alcohol, using drugs, crying, swearing, yelling, nervousness (nail-biting, pacing, fidgeting), changes in eating or sleeping habits.

Mental cues. Difficulty concentrating, decreased memory, indecisiveness, confusion, mind racing or going blank, decreased libido, inattentiveness, bad dreams, loss of sense of humor.

Emotional cues. Anxiety, anger, nervousness, depression, frustration, worry, fear, impatience, short temper, irritability.

Dr. Kelly described the college students he sees who are stressed out:

The students I usually see with stress related problems are generally healthy and happy individuals with active lifestyles. They may be concerned that their physical symptoms are caused by a virus or flulike illness, like mononucleosis, or even some other more serious illness. Occasionally these students become so distressed over the physical symptom that is caused by stress they get into a vicious cycle of worry.

They have a physical symptom that is real in every sense of the word. They have a real headache. They have real pain. It needs to be dealt with. Sometimes the solution is helping students look at their lifestyle and make appropriate changes.

So I ask, "Are you staying out late? Are you partying too much? Are you spending too much time studying in the library? When is the last time you exercised? Are you eating well? Are you using or abusing chemicals?" Sometimes a few meaningful changes in lifestyle have a tremendous impact on physical and mental well-being. (Kelly 2004)

Dr. Kelly also said that every student needs a good support system. At the minimum, this is having at least one person talk with. Having a friend or family member who will listen when you need to ventilate is a strategy for keeping mentally healthy. It is even better to have a network of friends, which might include a roommate, a new friend on campus, and an old high school buddy. If you can't talk about your feelings, you're on your way to becoming overstressed.

When Stress Becomes Generalized Anxiety Disorder

Everyone feels anxious from time to time from worrying about things that might happen. But students with chronic ongoing stress may have generalized anxiety disorder (GAD). This means they have physical symptoms that interfere with normal functioning. These physical signs can include restlessness, fatigue, problems with focus, and muscle tension. The diagnosis of generalized anxiety disorder is made when worrying gets out of control and makes one physically sick.

Generalized anxiety disorder often pairs with phobias, depression, irritable bowel syndrome, and relationship problems. Students who have GAD find they avoid others because of fear of rejection, or they may become dependent on someone else because of their lack of confidence.

The treatment for GAD is cognitive-behavioral therapy. In this method of treatment, a counselor helps you examine the causes of your condition and evaluate ways to respond. A therapist can help you examine the difference between productive and unproductive worrying and the costs and benefits of worrying. A counselor can also help you release worries using different methods. Sometimes therapists use muscle relaxation and breathing exercises to treat anxiety. Setting aside a "daily worry time" may also help. While medications are sometimes necessary, they may not be needed in every case. If you know you are a chronic worrier and worrying has started to affect your health, it makes sense to talk to a professional about the problem. You might feel pessimistic about the chances that anything will help you. It's true that you won't get better overnight. You will have to work to get better. But your counselor will help you keep track of your worries and practice different types of releases, and also coach you toward a place where you feel less burdened.

When Stress Is Really Depression

A recent American College Health Association survey found that more than 45 percent of college students have felt so depressed that they had difficulty functioning. In fact, more than a thousand college students commit suicide each year. Suicide is the third-leading cause of death among ten- to twenty-four-year-olds, and the numbers appear to be rising (National Institute of Mental Health 2004).

Feeling down and gloomy is a normal reaction to loss, life's struggles, or low self-esteem. But sometimes the feeling of sadness becomes intense, lasts for a long time, and prevents a person from leading a normal life. The good news is that depression is treatable. Unfortunately, most people never seek help.

Are you wondering if you are depressed? There are many instruments available to assess depression. These include online questionnaires at: www.webmd.com or at www.dbs alliance.org.

There are two general questions that family physicians use to screen for depression (Sharp 2002). These questions include, "Over the past two weeks, have you ever felt down, depressed, or hopeless?" and "Have you felt little interest or pleasure in doing things?" If the answer to these questions is yes, you may want to reflect on other signs and symptoms of depression. These include changes in sleep, eating, and mood patterns:

- *Changes in Sleep Patterns:* Having trouble falling asleep, waking up during the night, waking up early, or sleeping too much.
- *Changes in Eating Patterns:* Having no appetite, feeling hungry all the time, or experiencing weight loss or gain for no other obvious reason.
- *Changes in Mood:* Having feelings of sadness more than usual, having trouble focusing or making decisions, feeling sluggish or restless more than usual, or having no energy for daily activities.

Reflecting on these pattern changes can be insightful and may lead you to visit the health center or talk with a dorm or college counselor. Most importantly, if you have experienced any thoughts of harming yourself, you need to seek help immediately.

FINDING HELP FOR DEPRESSION

With the increasing occurrence of depression among college-age students, find out what your college is doing to cope with the problem. Make it a point to find out about student health services at your school. The health center may be a one-stop shop to attend classes, obtain preventive care, and also find help for acute illnesses. Where is the health clinic on your campus? Are there counselors on staff? How can a student be referred for specialized help? You or someone you know is bound to need to know about this resource. For instance, at the University of Iowa, the number of students treated at the Counseling Service center has doubled from 1,000 students a year to 2,300 a year in the past two decades (Schoon 2004). According to Sam Cochran, director of the service, it is not necessarily that students face more problems and challenges. Instead, the stigma of seeking assistance is diminishing and there are more effective treatments. Of the 2,300 initial consultations in the 2003-04 academic year, about a third continued in one-on-one counseling for an average of five sessions (Schoon 2004).

Normal Stress & Lifestyle Choices

Students with generalized anxiety disorder and depression need professional treatment. But some amount of stress is normal in college. It is important to manage all of the lifestyle stressors that are within your control. If you're not sleeping enough (see chapter 5), or if you're addicted to caffeine and/or nicotine, dealing with normal daily frustrations may cause undue stress.

It might seem like having a quick smoke to calm down is the answer. But smokers, don't fool yourself. The videos you saw in high school health class are realistic. The leading cancer killer of women is lung cancer. Smoking is especially dangerous for women, and the phenomenon is just beginning to be understood. Consider this statistic. Lung cancer in women has increased 600 percent since 1930 (Stabile 2005). The female hormone estrogen has something to do with the way cancer cells establish a home in the lungs. New therapies for lung cancer are based on blocking estrogen's role in tumor growth. Meanwhile, while the risk of a lung tumor seems a long way off when you are in college, smoking is neither glamorous nor a cool trick to unwind.

An exercise routine (see chapter 4) can help ward off everyday stress. Students need at least thirty minutes of vigorous exercise a day, whether from walking, running, skiing, playing basketball, lifting weights, or anything that gets your heart pumping fast. Exercise helps keep your circulation going and releases endorphins, which are, in simplest terms, natural roadblocks against depression and stress.

Coping with normal stress in college is all about finding a way to relax and let go. A state of mental calm allows your blood pressure to drop, your heart and breathing rate to slow down and your muscles to relax. You can practice the relaxation response on your own. When you find yourself burning up inside after a tiff with your roommate, try one of the simple ways to calm yourself discussed below.

MEDITATION

Meditation helps slow us down from the inside out. It is a method to reset your inner rhythm. Meditation is based on the verbal or silent repetition of a word, phrase, or mantra. This could be the words "love" or "peace on earth" or another comforting passage. To meditate, find a comfortable sitting position and rest your eyes. Beginning at your feet, consciously relax your muscles, moving next to your lower legs, upper legs, arms, abdomen, shoulders, and head. Take a breath slowly, and as you let it out, say the comforting words to yourself. Continue for five to ten minutes. This practice creates a relaxation response that can be measured by reduced oxygen consumption and slowed heart rate.

RHYTHMIC BREATHING

This is different than meditation. While you may practice rhythmic breathing while sitting, you can also do it while standing in line or lying in bed just before sleep. Simply take in a breath slowly, then count to five as you let the breath out. Continue this for five to ten minutes and notice yourself slowing down.

TIGHTEN & LET GO

Tensing and relaxing muscles is another simple and effective tool to reduce stress. It's easy. Find a quiet place to sit or lie down. Tense your whole body tightly by clenching your fists, wrinkling your face, and stretching your feet and arms. Count to ten as you hold your breath and keep this position. Now, relax gradually and let go of all the tension by letting go of your breath. Remain in the calm position for a minute. Repeat the process two more times, but use slightly less tension each time.

OTHER WAYS TO PHYSICALLY CALM DOWN

Consciously relaxing to reduce stress and its negative side effects is a behavior that you can learn to do. Consider the many activities that may induce calmness for you: a brisk walk, listening to a symphony in candlelight, taking a hot bubble bath, calling your grandma, reading poetry, or playing the harmonica.

Emotions are not isolated experiences. They are triggered by our perception of events. When we consciously chill out, it is easier to choose to think positive thoughts rather than negative thoughts, and loving thoughts rather than hateful thoughts. The thoughts we choose dictate our emotional response.

LEARNING TO FORGIVE

Is there someone you need to forgive? Are you holding on to anger with your mom, roommate, or girlfriend? Let's just face this question honestly. Is your resentment and anxiety going to change anything? Holding on to a grudge and not letting go of rage results in physical symptoms. These include increased blood pressure, hormone changes, and depressed immune response. Learning to forgive big and little things works to reduce stress in several ways.

Studies show people in troubled relationships have higher levels of cortisol, a hormone associated with impaired immune function (Lewis and Adler 2004). Everett Worthington is the Executive Director of A Campaign for Forgiveness Research. He says, "Every time you feel unforgiveness, you are more likely to develop a health problem."

Choosing to forgive in order to restore a treasured relationship is always worth it. In college, you may still be moving from an immature pattern to a mature pattern of learning how to love unconditionally.

All relationships experience hurt. But it is not practical to discard friendships whenever there is a rift. In fact, relationships grow stronger when conflicts are bridged. Remember that peacemaking is not always about giving in or allowing someone to walk over you. Rather, peacemaking is the art of taking the initiative to resolve troubles, even if you end up agreeing to disagree about an issue with someone you care about. It may be as simple as you being the first to say, "I don't like the way we're relating. Can we talk about things?" And if you need help forgiving a deep hurt, talk it out with a friend or a counselor or ask for guidance through prayer.

WHEN STRESS HITS YOU IN THE GUT

When you panic over an Education Methods project due in two days, your stomach tightens, your intestines twist, and before you know it, you are racing to a bathroom. Gastrointestinal problems—everything from heartburn to irritable bowel syndrome —go along with stress in college.

The brain and digestive system are well connected. Nervous diarrhea is caused by uncontrolled contractions in the lower gastrointestinal tract. The nervous system, hormones, and electrical impulses in the colon may trigger this unwelcome feeling. If the condition of nervous diarrhea continues, it may be diagnosed as Irritable Bowel Syndrome (IBS). Other common digestive symptoms that may suggest IBS include alternating constipation and nervous diarrhea, stomach pain, bloating, or feeling an urgency to have a bowel movement.

Scientists at the University of North Carolina (Cahill 2004) found that cognitive behavioral therapy was most helpful in treating an irritable bowel. When the brain perceives pain, it tends to fret over the sensation and thus, makes it bigger. In cognitive behavioral therapy, a trained counselor helps patients stop that cycle from starting by saying to themselves, "I can manage this pain." In the study, 70 percent of patients reported less pain and diarrhea after twelve weeks, compared with about 40 percent who only received literature about the condition.

INTERNET STRESS & INSTANT MESSAGING

One of the stressors your parents didn't have to deal with as college students back in the 1970s was the stress of the Internet. Whether instant messaging or hanging around in online video game rooms, glassy-eyed students sometimes can't walk away. When does harmless Internet surfing cross into overuse or become an addiction?

Nathan A. Shapira, MD, Ph.D., a psychiatrist in the McKnight Brain Institute at the University of Florida in Gainesville, has been studying this social problem. He reports, "Many people use the computer to satisfy, stir up excitement, release tension, or provide relief—whether it involves sex or not. Surfing, chatting, playing interactive games—that's where those long hours go. It's just that when Internet use becomes excessive, it can—like other impulse disorders— be distressing and disabling" (Shapira et al. 2003).

Internet overuse is a psychological dependence. The same thing can happen with food, exercise, sex, or gambling. Internet abuse often affects the same students who compulsively shop. Depression also seems to lead others to overuse, creating a vicious cycle fed by isolation. Here are some signs of a serious Internet problem:

- A preoccupation in which the Internet becomes irresistible.
- Use of the Internet for longer periods than planned.
- A preoccupation that causes significant problems in relationships, work, or other important areas of functioning.
- The person tries to cut back but can't.

- The person gets a sense of tension or arousal before going online and seems to experience pleasure afterward—much as kleptomaniacs feel after stealing something.
- The person neglects other responsibilities, such as assignments and deadlines.

Cognitive behavioral therapy—which involves learning how to deal with feelings that lead to excessive Internet use—helps people control their urges and manage their time better. Medications may also help.

Financial Stressors

Most college students experience some financial pressure. For instance, in order to pay tuition, you may have to work twenty hours a week. With the demands of your work-study or off-campus job, you fall behind in the classroom. Now you have two large stresses weighing on your shoulders. And sometimes you can't drop the most difficult class, or you'll wind up losing financial aid. Don't panic. Look at all the options. Can you drop a nonessential class? Can you get aid from a different source, whether through a loan or from your family? Talk with your personal banker or someone at the financial aid office before it becomes a crisis. Level with your academic counselor, your professors, and, most importantly, your family. They are there to help. Taking fewer classes, finding another job, or graduating a bit later may all be reasonable solutions.

Spiritual Support & Emotional Health

In a major national study relating college students' religious practices to their psychological well-being, social scientist Alexander Astin surveyed students at forty-six colleges. He found that those who participated in religious activities were more likely to have higher scores for emotional and mental health than students who had no religious involvement. Astin found that 7 percent of college students prayed, 78 percent discussed religion with friends, and 76 percent were searching for meaning and purpose in life (Hofius 2004).

During your most stressful moments, you might consider prayer, Bible study, or worship. Students surveyed for this book reported a range of feelings about spirituality and also chose different means to connect to their spiritual beliefs.

It is normal for young people to have many feelings about spirituality; a variety of spiritual styles exists to speak to wherever you are in your spiritual development. A high degree of spirituality correlates with high self-esteem and feeling good about the direction your life is headed. The study mentioned above defined spirituality as the desire to integrate spirituality into life, the belief that people are spiritual beings, and the belief in the sacredness of life and that people have spiritual experiences.

Guess why discussing spirituality is important? Astin, the study's principal

what students said:

I strayed from all things religious. After attending a Catholic high school, I didn't like the services on campus.

The time I connect with God is in listening to and singing praise music and in my daily quiet times. My friends at college have influenced this by keeping me on track and accountable.

I was involved in Bible study and also read on my own. I attended chapel almost every day.

I have been reading The Purpose-driven Life.

I attended daily chapel at the beginning of the year, but I stopped going in order to do more homework and sleep.

Our praise and worship service was awesome and I love to sing, so it was really enjoyable.

I wish I would have been involved in Bible study.

I found the churches off campus very impersonal, and I felt awkward being there.

investigator, said it is normal and expected for psychological well-being to decline during the college years. He even reported that three-quarters of college juniors report feeling depressed frequently or occasionally (Hofius 2004).

The study also found a link between spiritual practices and substance use. Three-fourths of students who don't drink beer before attending college won't start in college if involved in religious activity, but only 46 percent of students will abstain if not involved religiously.

If you're feeling stressed-out and are not connected to a spiritual practice or community, maybe it is time to check out a faith-based group on your campus.

Fifty Ways to Deal with Stress in College

Now that you understand why stress is a universal college experience and how it can lead to serious health issues, look through this list of fifty healthy ways to relieve it.

PHYSICAL RELEASES

Moving your body has been a natural stress release since you were born. Remember playing hide-and-seek while waiting in the doctor's office? Physical movement releases nervous energy, tension, and frustration. By stretching, bending, and moving your arms and legs, you will feel loose, energized, and reborn.

While some of the sports and activities discussed on the following pages are in the mainstream, others are not. Take the old notion of "Go outside and play." This idea can include pounding a tetherball, swimming in a river, walking along a nature path, or playing paintball. Find a buddy to go for a run or a walk with you. A running partner may also turn out to be a confidant, so talk about what is bugging you during that last half mile back to your dorm.

1. Moonlight runs. Yes, moonlight runs! Go with a partner, choose a safe, well-lit, well-traveled route, and discover how running in the moonlight is an exhilarating experience.

2. Biking. Mountain biking, speed biking, or just taking a leisurely pedal around a

Christa, an elementary ed major from Iowa: *Every morning and every night my roommate would wake up and do yoga stretches. For her it performed two completely different releases, depending on the time of day. In the morning it would help her to wake up and get her muscles going, and at night it would relax her breathing and help her focus on sleeping well.*

Kristy, who is also a resident advisor, tested the stress releases for this book: *One of my favorite stress releases was going sledding with residents on my floor. This is a great way to get out and enjoy the fresh air, and it is actually a workout running up and down the hill.*

new corner. You don't have to be Lance Armstrong to feel stress disappear through those rolling wheels.

3. Volleyball. Volleyball requires jumping, running, bending, and constant focus. That white ball can represent your worries as you pound it up and away.

4. Dodgeball. If you can't release stress by hurling a rubber ball as hard as you can at some of your best friends, then physical release just may not work for you.

5. Free weights. Keep a set of weights under your bed and take ten to twenty minutes to lift between study assignments.

6. Snowball fights. This one will require you to live in an area that actually experiences snow. But if you do, they are great fun. This activity is similar to dodgeball, but with an endless supply of ammunition. Snowball fights also require constant movement, just to avoid freezing.

7. Splashing in the rain. Grab some old shoes and watch out for lightning as you pop up the umbrella and enter the symphony of a rainstorm. You probably remember a gym class or athletic practice in the rain. It probably felt like playing on a giant Slip 'N Slide. Running in the rain gives you a feeling of freedom.

8. Basketball. In the gym or on the outdoor court, it's a game anyone can pick up to get away from it all. Basketball is also a great team game, so if you want to talk about how much you dislike your psych professor while making a layup, all the better.

9. Rhythmic breathing. Become aware of your breath coming in and going out. Count to five as you inhale—then let it go slowly. Feel more centered.

10. Become well-read. Most colleges have major national and international newspapers in the library. Find a comfy quiet corner and chill out with the *London Times*, *San Francisco Chronicle*, *New York Times*, or *Chicago Tribune*.

11. Sledding. For about ten dollars, you can purchase an inflatable sled and go flying down your favorite campus hillside.

SOCIAL RELEASES

You were probably involved in a club or social group during high school. It might have been student government, the marching band, or the drama group. In college, experiences like these don't come looking for you. You have to go out and ask to participate! But the clubs and committees at most colleges will probably outnumber those you had to choose from in high school. Got a passion for photography? There is a club for you. Crazy about cooking? There may be classes offered at the local food co-op. And if there isn't a club to support your fascination with insects, then start one! Most colleges allow students to create a group, as long as you request permission to advertise it through the college. If there is something that you

Sasha, a business major from Minnesota: *My own release was found after taking a class. Many would find it odd to lie on the floor and 'just breathe,' but from my Intro to Theatre and Dance Class (although quite uncomfortable and different at first), it became something that I enjoy doing. When I am regulating my breathing, I am also keeping a close connection to my body's basic involuntary actions. It's comforting to take a step back and think about the basic human breath. It's relaxing to turn on some easy music and take the time to just breathe. Then, after ten minutes I think about what I have planned for the next day and how I am going to face any challenges that I will have.*

Pete signed up for a Certified Nursing Assistant course at a care center: *The class has allowed me to appreciate my youth and identify the needs of the elderly. It keeps me busy. I am always on my feet, and it has increased my ability to provide sympathy to others.*

are quite passionate about, why not throw the idea out there? Having this kind of release is the best, because you'll be able to immerse yourself in your passion with others who care as much as you do.

12. Volunteer for an organization or cause. It is never too early or too late to discover the payback of helping others. Freshman year in college may be the time for you. There are always organizations, both on and off campus, looking for help. If you're interested in kids, volunteer as a coach in a softball league or as a tutor in a local elementary school. Do you enjoy talking with senior citizens? There is probably a care center close by with needs for letter writers and readers. Teaching someone else is the highest form of learning. And besides, it's good for your ego. It just feels good helping someone else.

13. Join a council. If you find an established council that interests you, then sign up! Remember, in high school others always brought the opportunities to you. In college, you have to make an effort to be a part of them.

MUSICAL RELEASES

Music is recognized for its therapeutic value everywhere from the operating room to the counselor's office. According to the American Music Therapy Association (2006), music helps alleviate pain and promote wellness, expression of feelings, and memory. Whether it's punk rock on your mp3 player, singing in the shower or playing classical guitar in the dorm room, consider all of the ways that music can help you release stress.

14. Learn a new instrument. Why not? Take a piano or guitar class. Maybe you took piano lessons as a kid and gave them up. Wouldn't you love to pound away on something from Coldplay or Ben Folds? What about the guitar? It is never too late to form your own band.

15. Join a musical group, or form one. Once you've learned an instrument, or found friends who share your passion for sound, take it up a step! Select music that makes you feel happy when you perform it, and then show people! Go to clubs or college talent shows. Even singing in the dorm lobby is a fun way to release stress. The University of Iowa has an open mike night a few times a month where people can go and perform; you can tell that the musicians really enjoy themselves, no matter what the crowd's reaction is.

16. Sing, anywhere. Singing is a great release. Anyone reading this book who says they haven't ever sung along to their favorite song in the shower is probably fibbing. You can lose yourself in whatever you're singing about.

17. Write music. Writing music is an incredible release of stress because you can put your feelings down on a piece of paper and work away at them. Whether you're pounding out a guitar melody or reworking a line,

Brad tested the CD review/swapping club strategy: *Instead of actually swapping CDs, I just talked to a couple of friends and had them tell me about some of their favorite bands and songs. I would then add those songs to my music library. I thought that this music thing was an excellent stress release. When I felt stressed, I would just sit down at my computer and listen to some of these songs. That made me feel a lot better. So, this program definitely helped "strangle my stress."*

stress can disappear through the music. Writing new words to your favorite song is also a lot of fun.

18. CD review/swapping club. At any college, you're going to hear a lot of different kinds of music playing from the dorm rooms. Take a stroll and listen for rap, rock, country, classical, and pop music. Maybe it is time to explore a new genre by borrowing a friend's country CD and loaning them a few of your punk favorites. Get together and talk about different musical tastes. Sharing makes a swapping club discussion session so much fun!

SPIRITUAL RELEASES

Religion and faith are a somewhat forgotten dimension of college student life. When you go to college, you may be thankful to sleep in on Sunday mornings. No one will be telling you to get dressed for church. On the other hand, some of you will relish the fact that, in college, you'll meet lots of people who share your very active faith. No matter which side of that fence you're on, talking to God or your spiritual deity about your problems, stresses, and struggles is a huge relief.

What does behavioral science say about college students going to church? A study at UCLA found nonchurchgoing students are more than twice as likely to feel depressed as those who attend services frequently. Of the surveyed students who attended worship, joined a campus religious group, or read sacred texts, fewer reported feeling overwhelmed or stressed compared to those who did not have these habits (Hofius 2004). Here are several ways to connect with your spirituality.

19. Faith-based clubs. Groups like Chabad or Hillel can be another outlet. Often, these groups are more like get-togethers for people of like faith to play guitar, sing, and talk about life. These groups give you the opportunity to interact with other people who have a similar faith relationship.

20. Wear your spirituality. In whatever context you find a relationship to the spirit, there will probably be bracelets, shirts, or necklaces to reflect and validate this important value in your life. Go ahead and wear them.

21. Prayer. Whether or not you had a prayer routine at home, consider starting one now. Some students pray before going

Frank, who sings in the choir and comes from Iowa, tried out the wear your spirituality strategy: *I had a problem with a temper, whether it was in schoolwork, on the golf course, or being stressed-out in the dorm room. On a whim, I went into a Christian bookstore and bought a black WWJD (What Would Jesus Do) bracelet. At first, I felt somewhat self-conscious. But I noticed that a lot of people wore them, friends and teachers alike. Anytime I felt stressed-out or I wanted to explode, I would look at the bracelet and I would calm down and find another outlet. That bracelet was the only thing that never left my body last year. I wore it everywhere, and it's pretty beaten and dirty now, but it's more valuable to me than almost anything because of the comfort it's brought me.*

to bed and even fall asleep in the middle of prayers. Praying before sleep is a way to talk about what is going on with your life, and to ask for blessings and protection of those close to you.

22. Read the Koran or the Torah. You don't have to start in the beginnning. But finding passages that speak to you can be an incredible tool for peacefulness. Consider a verse in the Christian Bible from 1 Peter 5:7: "Cast all your anxieties unto him, because he cares for you."

PERSONAL RITUALS

Taking time to care for your body enriches your mind. Keeping your room and car free of empty pizza boxes and old receipts enhances your productivity. In this section, you will find a new slant on old routines that can help you release anxiety.

23. Take a shower. Yes, shower. A simple shower can do wonders for your body. When your body feels physically tense, whether in the shoulders or neck, or if you have a headache, put down your book and pick up a towel.

24. Manicures/Pedicures. At the end of a long week or a rough day, you can arrange an inexpensive spa treatment at the local college of cosmetology and feel pampered for pennies.

25. Create a new style. When you're with friends who are experiencing the same stresses you are, define a new trend. You can all agree to wear mismatched socks the next day to class.

26. Clean your dorm room. It's not the first release you'd think of, but it's a great one. It is normal to feel more anxious as your room goes from orderly to a pigsty. By organizing your papers, putting away your laundry, and vacuuming the floor, you can feel like you are washing, dusting, and polishing all the stuff you are worried about.

27. Wash your car. The same principle applies here. When you don't feel like studying anymore, take your car to the car wash. You can wash worries about that upcoming accounting test away. And you will have a great looking car, to boot.

28. Stargaze. Stargazing is not only a great date, it's a nice way to realize what's around us. When you get caught up in your routine, go outside at night, sit on a bench, and look up at the stars. Seeing their distant light helps you forget your worries, at least for a while.

29. Have a picnic. It doesn't even have to be outdoors! The beauty of picnics is that they can be anytime, anywhere. If everyone chips in, it can be a banquet, even in the middle of the dorm room.

30. Take a ride. An open road and some great music can help you leave your troubles behind. Cruise down a dark highway with all the windows open, singing a favorite song at the top of your lungs. Invite a friend who might enjoy the change of scenery to join you.

Christa, who loves to experiment with new looks, tested the manicures/pedicures stress release: *Now when I get my hair done each month, I get a manicure. It's a perfect use of time while my hair dye is setting, and it is a nice way to feel pampered without spending that much money. I love it!*

31. Write a letter. Writing letters is a dying art in the age of cell phones, e-mail, and pagers. A handwritten letter is a great way to release stress. If you really want to contact a friend you haven't talked to in a while, go on the Internet and find his or her address. Reaching into your mailbox and finding a letter is always a nice surprise, but when it's from a friend you haven't heard from in a while, it's even better. It seems more meaningful to get a letter that you can hold. When was the last time you got an e-mail that you really wanted to print out to keep forever?

32. Journal. Writing in a journal is an age-old release. Record the ups and downs of your day. Doing so helps you realize that maybe your day wasn't as awful as you thought, or it can remind you of a happy event coming up in the future. You can also go back and read the old entries to remember good times. Either way, when you journal, you get thoughts out of your head and down on paper.

33. Call family. It sounds like the easy way out, but calling your parents and siblings is a wonderful release. Look at it this way: Calling your parents makes them happy. It enables them to keep up with how you're doing in college. Giving them a call is a way for them to keep up with the little changes. And chances are, if you're struggling to get through your college math class, they can sympathize. It's great to talk to your siblings as well. It's a wonderful break from your responsibilities to talk with your little brother or sister and plan for an upcoming event—like the next holiday visit or going to a concert or movie together.

34. Conversation sessions/message boards. Message boards are a great way to communicate with your friends. Leaving encouraging notes is a way to help one another get through the rough times.

SIT, LISTEN & OBSERVE

Okay, all these activities can't be "get up and go" ideas, because there are just times when you want to sit down and rest. Here are a few options.

35. Cook. When you get frustrated with the world, check out the dorm-style recipes in this book and mix something up. Once you're energized from the food and the creative endeavor, you'll be ready to deal with whatever is bothering you.

36. Create a "finished" list. Finished lists can be uplifting reflections. Here is one approach: Find a large pad and record everything you want to do for the day, from marketing presentations to brushing your teeth. By writing everything down then crossing off completed tasks, you get a feeling of accomplishment.

37. Watch TV. Enough said. Watching TV is permissible, enjoyable, and entertaining, as long as you don't overdo it. How much is too much? Decide for yourself, and then observe your own rule.

38. Daily quiet time. Maybe you once dreaded quiet time. But in college, it is a glorious experience. It only comes along once in a while, and it is very valuable.

Laura, who used the daily quiet time strategy: *My roommate and I spent many a night listening to my dolphin noise CD. It was very relaxing. And we also found a hypnosis CD and that actually worked. We meditated too. Either way, we would concentrate on quiet, restful sounds, that took over our entire body, and both of us were the better for it.*

Establishing regular quiet time can be therapeutic when you feel rushed during the day. Quiet time is just that—quiet. No Comedy Central. No music. Just you and your favorite novel or magazine. Silence is very calming.

39. Don't end your day with homework. Let's be real: Unless you're really into studying, there are things you would rather do. So, don't end your day with it! Always unwind for at least fifteen minutes at the end of each day with a peaceful activity—whether it is watching late-night talk shows or taking a nice hot bath.

CHILDHOOD ACTIVITIES

Don't be afraid to go to back to your childhood experiences when you're stressed-out. We're not talking about Sesame Street shows. We're talking about childhood behaviors. Children laugh naturally and often. What about you? Here are ways to find the kid in you again.

40. Whistling. Kids really celebrate when they finally learn to whistle. As we grow older, we become shy about whistling for fear of embarrassment. It's too bad. Whistling is something that can lift your spirits and make you feel good. And whistling is impossible to do unless your face and muscles are relaxed, which makes it a great stress reliever.

41. Take a detour. When you're outdoors, watch kids meander down a sidewalk or wander through a mall. Unless they're being held, children never go in a straight line—they go every which way they please. We can learn from them. Life is not meant to be lived on a straight line—it is sometimes random. Kids understand this reality, and as the stress of college piles up, we forget it.

42. Discover new colors. Color will affect your mood. So why settle for drab hues? Don't settle for muted tones of browns and flesh colors. What happened to candy apple red? Spice your life up with some color in your wardrobe, your room, or even your hair!

43. Become an artist. Remember finger painting? Think of how proud you were to create a picture when you were in first grade, even if you look at it now and shudder. The point is that kids do things for enjoyment, not results. For them, it is fun. It's relaxing. It is a way to express feelings. Go ahead and do the same! Use art to express the tension or feelings that you're holding inside.

BE CREATIVE

Perhaps after your long days in the biology lab, your creative brain cells have gone to sleep. Release the tension of rote memory exercise by energizing that other side of your cranium.

44. Develop a celebration routine. When you're finished with work, make sure that you have a signal to show yourself that you have completed whatever you've been doing. Select a "trigger" to tell yourself that you're done with your responsibilities and ready to move on to something else. Here are some activities to help push you into a fun gear.

Laura, a music major: *On a specific note, during study time for finals, my roommate, a couple of our neighbors, and I cranked up my ten-year-old Spice Girls CD and jumped on her mattress while screaming at the top of our lungs. That's a little extreme, but hey, something needed to be done . . . It was stressful.*

- Finish your daily errands on the way back to your residence.
- Run around the block.
- Do a quick burst of exercise.
- Take off your work clothes.
- Take a shower.
- Have a snack.
- Watch your favorite television program.

45. Invent a new competition. Yes, a new contest, something as simple as folding paper airplanes. A new sport will take the help of some of your friends, but it can be a ton of fun. Or play "trash ball," which is putting the trash can in the hallway and throwing foam balls inside for a score. This may even draw a crowd, creating a natural opportunity to socialize during a study break.

46. Celebrate holidays. Carve a pumpkin. Put up a Christmas tree. Send valentines. There are many holidays during the college academic year that offer these opportunities.

47. Random acts of kindness. Send friends random notes, or share food treats. Offer your neighbor some leftover pizza.

48. Learn odd facts or master jokes. Did you know that a sneeze leaves your nose at one hundred miles per hour? Or that Americans choke on toothpicks more than anything else? Laughter is always a great way to release stress.

49. Learn a new language. Go online and study conversational French. You'll feel a little like you're in Paris.

50. Take time to create a thoughtfulness calendar. Imagine how thrilled your aunt would be to receive an online birthday greeting from her niece in college.

When Things Go Wrong . . .

Obviously, even when you're trying to de-stress, things can still go wrong. Thankfully, there are always ways to make yourself feel better, even during an emergency. Here are our favorite nerve-saving tips:

- Take a deep breath, slow down, then take another.
- Count to ten slowly.
- Talk to yourself: "Hang in there," "You can do it," "When the going gets tough . . ."
- Think about the best outcome possible.
- Look for the lesson inside your problem.
- Take a five-minute break and make a new plan.
- Remind yourself that when you are eighty years old and rocking your great-grandchild to sleep, this problem will probably be lost forever in your memory.

Stress can get to anyone. It's only human nature. But the good thing about stress is that it can be controlled, and even eliminated, if you have the right releases for it. Hopefully this chapter has given you more than one creative way to cope the next time you're feeling the pressure!

how to stay organized

In college, you will feel busier than in high school. It's just that there are so many things you will be managing. You will be living without daily parental guidance for possibly the first time in your life. On one hand, you will be able to have friends over whenever you want, listen to your music at full volume, and sleep until noon on Saturday. But all of those choices can get in the way of the outcome you are paying an institution to provide—to discover new knowledge, earn a degree, and start a personally rewarding career.

As an incoming college student, it's likely that you'll encounter the same problems as the students we interviewed. The good thing is that there is always something you can do to manage your time better. All of those problems have solutions, and any situation you think is too complex to manage can be changed. First, we need to look at how to become organized, and then, how to stay that way for the rest of the year. Staying organized requires a system, your own personal way of making sense of it all, your own unique way to keep order. After all, organization is little more than keeping track of what is important. To keep yourself on task, you just need to focus on how all the little things fit together. We'll help you by covering the following issues in this chapter:

- Separating socializing from studying
- Making your room a study place
- Waking up and staying up
- Cramming and other bad study habits
- Playing and studying on weekends
- Confronting procrastination
- Keeping yourself on task

That's a big list. But just keep reading.

Creating Time for Everything

Managing your time is going to be the only way you get that Invertebrate Biology chapter outlined before you achieve a good night's rest. Organization is much tougher in college than it was in high school. Part of the reason is that you will have much more to do—like keeping up with laundry, paying bills, and remembering all of your academic commitments. The other problem is that—seemingly overnight—you have become your own

what students said:

It was tough to motivate myself to work.

I'm easily distracted.

I procrastinate on everything.

How do I make time for work, friends, and classes?

Weekends flew by without me working at all.

I have too many things to organize at once.

If people would just get into a routine, right away, it would make all the difference. A routine doesn't leave room for wasting time.

boss and you don't have anyone around telling you what to do. This is both a privilege and problem. In college, the teachers will expect you to keep up with the assignments on your own, rather than force you to read and discuss american politics out loud as you did in high school. If you don't want to read a chapter, you won't have to. No one is going to force you. And why stop there—if you don't want to attend class, you won't have to! No one is going to send a tardy notice to your mom. The same goes for paying bills.

Without supervision from parents, teachers, or relatives, you will be free to do as much, or rather as little, as you choose. The results can be scary. It sounds fun to dream, "No homework? No responsibility? Where do I sign up?" But when your grades sink, your bills and interest charges pile up, and you don't have any way to fix things fast, you will be in a very distressing situation.

Luckily, this chapter is designed to help you avoid all that. To keep yourself on task, however, you'll have to start some new habits the second that you walk into your dorm.

Begin by Creating a List

A diary or notebook can be a great help. At the beginning of each day, write down exactly every single task that you must accomplish during the day. OK, now you're started. Making the list is simple enough; now let's look at a timeline.

Along with each task, write down when you will tend to that task. This works well for people who are very good at judging the amount of time each task will require. But for others, estimating leads to frustration, because by midmorning they are already behind and feeling negative about their list. Another strategy is to simply assign a priority value to each task. Label high priority tasks with an A. A tasks are vital and absolutely necessary for you to accomplish that day. Plan your schedule around those high-priority tasks. B tasks are the ones that need to be completed, but if need be they could be rescheduled without much trouble. Label optional tasks C. They are tasks you would like to do, but if they are not done at the end of the day, you won't suffer serious consequences. Stars (*) can also be used for this prioritization of tasks, with three stars being tasks that must be accomplished that day.

Be sure to celebrate and recognize when something is accomplished by crossing it off the list or making a check mark next to it. Continue adding to the list the next day, and consider whether you need to designate any of yesterday's B tasks as A tasks. At the end of the day, simply reflect on all that you have completed during the day, and reward yourself for the goals you have accomplished.

Choose Your Study Haven

At home, you probably did homework in three places—in front of the TV, on the kitchen counter, or in your bedroom. Unfortunately, in college these three places are often in the same room! You won't have the same level of privacy and comfort in your dorm to study, so you'll have to make a choice. Here are the most common options:

- *Study in the dorm,* which may require an understanding between you and your roommate about the times when homework can be done.
- *Study in the library,* where you're guaranteed quiet, peace of mind, and fewer distractions.
- *Study in and around quiet nooks on campus,* which can give you the most peace and freedom to roam around but leaves you subject

to the unexpected—like someone else claiming your shade tree behind the science building.

- *Become flexible and use a variety of places.*

Any of these choices will work, and you can decide which one works for you on any given day. It's just that it's another decision you'll have to make, instead of being a creature of routine. Let's look at each option, one by one, and discuss the pros and cons of each.

IN YOUR ROOM

Pros: For starters, your dorm room is the easiest of the four locations. After all, you're already living in your dorm room, so you don't have to make an effort to find an empty bench or walk through the rain to the library. Your dorm room is also the easiest place for you to find a comfortable spot, secure a computer, and control the noise. For instance, you can't listen to your music in the library unless you have a high-end pair of headphones. In your room, you can listen to your music, type up your French assignment on the computer, and eat a snack at the same time.

Cons: If you're chilled out on the bed or couch, listening to music, and eating baked potato chips while preparing for an economics quiz, you may not get as much work done. Also, unless you arrange otherwise, your roommate may be in the room at the same time as you. If your roommate wants to watch *The O.C.*, it will be nearly impossible for you to study for that killer quiz without glancing up at the screen every two minutes.

To make sure you're getting to work, you'll need to develop a system for nurturing a work environment. Consider these rituals and signals to help you stay focused:

- Listen for the closing music of a morning TV show to indicate it is time to get to work.
- Turn off all distractions, like the CD player.
- Turn on your computer.
- Pour a glass of your favorite "get to work" drink.
- Set an alarm to go off when it is time to work.

IN THE LIBRARY

Pros: Honestly, what says "studying efficiently" more than a library? All the books and electronic resources of the campus will be at your fingertips. Every room will be quiet, so people will know not to bother you. Some professors have offices in or near the library as well, so they can be handy for help on an assignment. Most professors love to talk to concerned students, and studying in a place close to your teachers makes communicating with them easier.

Cons: Personal freedom in the library is very limited. If you like to listen to music when you study, this can be a problem. A lot of libraries won't allow headphones or cell phones inside the building. You will have to watch other people around you to be sure you are not bothering anyone. You'll be limited in your ability to express yourself as well. If you're having a bad day and you feel like going off on a rant about your philosophy teacher, you'll be potentially disturbing a quiet space. The final downside about the library is that it can be inconvenient to get to. It isn't fun lugging fifteen pounds of textbooks for twenty minutes to find a quiet work space. If you want to compose something and you don't have a laptop, it's not as though you can haul your computer into the building. You might have to compose the paper on a library desktop computer and then e-mail it back to your dorm room. And be careful about cruising to those online chat rooms while on the computer in the library. You might tell yourself that you're working, but you will burn up your study time on the blog in a hurry.

AROUND CAMPUS

Pros: Choosing different quiet corners provides some variety, and that's a plus. You can find a different place to study every day if you like. Selecting a comfy lounge chair outside the campus auditorium to read your Spanish assignment is very relaxing. If you want to create a study group of friends who meet on the benches outside the gym to talk about argumentation strategies, you'll have that freedom as well. Or if you want to study in a crowded place, like a coffee shop, to meet new people as well as get a little work done, that's another choice.

Cons: If you are planning on combining socializing with studying, just figure that you're not going to be maximally productive. Hanging out in the dining hall is a fine way to make new friends while studying. But you'll need to monitor your progress on pages actually read and worksheets actually done, especially if the only reason you're camping out at a table is to watch for that hottie from your biology lab. Studying around campus also leaves you subject to whatever events are taking place at the time. If the restaurant you study in is having a live band that night, you're out of luck, and windy days and rain can wreck any plans for outdoor study.

BECOME FLEXIBLE

Pros: By choosing to be flexible, you'll be telling yourself that you will study hard when you need to, whether you're in your dorm room, around campus, or in the library. Being flexible will allow you many opportunities for creative learning. If you're having a serious finals study session, a group of friends in the library can be fun. If you're watching the movie version of a book you're reading for your English class, then the dorm is a perfect spot. By keeping yourself open, you'll be able to study wherever is most convenient and efficient at the time. And you won't get bored with the same study environment.

Cons: Unfortunately, by leaving yourself open and flexible, your study can be disrupted. For example, if you plan on studying in the library at seven that night but decide to do it in your room instead, you might come home to find your roommate playing video games. Before long, you'll be holding a joystick instead of a textbook. That's not good. Having flexible plans with others can mean time lost as well. When half of the group is used to meeting in the library and the other half thinks the session will take place in someone's dorm room, you can waste as much time trying to find your partners as you spend actually learning.

Each study situation has its own benefits and drawbacks. Before you go to school or in the first week, think about how each choice would work for you. Be honest with yourself. If you know you can't study around a TV, plan on studying outside your room for the vast majority of time. If you like to be by yourself when you study, then find a nice spot on campus where you're totally alone. It will probably be a forgotten corner of the library—but that's okay. If you get more done by multitasking, then stay in the dorms. And if you prefer to do things with groups, or prefer to just see what happens, then stay flexible. By taking an honest approach and continually analyzing your study environments, you will keep a check on yourself and continually improve your prospects of achieving academic success.

Cramming & Other Nasty Study Habits

Cramming is a trick everyone has probably tried at least once in their life. Cramming is a skill that is somewhat useful in high school, when you're learning new chapters every month. In college, where you're consuming the same volume of information in a week and then being tested, it is next to impossible to cram.

Cramming is also a horrible habit to get into for another reason—finals. Most finals, and even midterms, are comprehensive. If you're only learning the material the night before your routine exams, chances are that you'll forget it just as quickly. By the time those big tests come along, you'll be starting over and there simply won't be enough time. Then you may panic. And that doesn't bode well for a good grade point average. To avoid cramming, you're going to have to recognize that work and assignments pile up quickly and there is less "in between" time.

Remember how it was in high school? If you didn't complete an assignment in class, there was almost always a study hall later in the day. You were able to head home most nights without a lot of books because your work had been completed in the classroom. Well . . . college isn't like that—at all!

In college, even though the classes will be longer than in high school, the teachers will spend nearly every minute talking about the reading assignment. The very last few minutes of the class period might be spent on giving an example from the next day's homework. You're on your own—to read, to decide what is important, and to know how you are going to remember it.

The other problem that occurs is that, much like in high school, you're dashing from class to class during the day. But, unlike high school, you're not getting any homework done during classes. By the time you finally make it back to your dorm room to start your homework, you can have five or six assignments swimming around in your head, and you might not have started any of them. Trying to calculate a statistics problem while you're trying to remember a sequence from your chemistry class—before you forget them both—is an ordeal. Because of the new pace and work volume in college, you'll need some new ways to manage. Here are a few helpful approaches.

SCHEDULE BREAKS IN THE DAY

It is not fun having five classes back-to-back in college. It doesn't seem like much in elementary school, but when you're lugging books for five college classes around it's tiring. Take three classes in a row, at most, and then schedule an hour to grab something to eat and review your assignments or start some homework. You might need a break just to run back to the dorm to get materials for the rest of your day. That hour or two will help you renew your energy and manage your materials.

RENEW YOUR ENERGY

Sometimes you need to get away from the mental stress of classes that require a lot of memorization, like Plant Biology. Remember the cell phone analogy in our sleep chapter? Your brain can just feel fried from trying to remember too many facts at once. By scheduling a break, you'll recoup some energy. Give yourself time to recover and recharge your battery.

MANAGE YOUR MATERIALS

College textbooks are large and heavy. And for a lot of classes, you're not going to have just one book. Fred's freshman English class covered over fifteen different books in the first semester alone! That was only one class. If you're taking three or four classes a day, you might end up carrying ten books on your back. Unless you plan on lugging a suitcase into your lectures, you won't be able to do it. Plan a break in the day to go back to the dorm and "reload your supplies."

If you schedule a break in the day and you aren't tired, or if you have all the books you need with you already, then you can put your time to use for the most important reason that you're at college—to learn! If you schedule a free hour between classes, use that time to your advantage. Work on the calculus problem that stumped you in class, or catch up on the questions from Russian Literature. You can also use your free time to visit your professors if they aren't teaching another class. Most professors have office hours during the day when you can drop in for some help. Imagine—a break in the day, and some personal help from your instructor! It's all part of feeling organized.

It is very easy to read this book and tell yourself that you're going to work hard anytime you get the chance. But before long, you're going to experience a behavior that all college students struggle with—it starts with a P.

Procrastination Affects Everyone

You know about procrastination from high school, but it rises to a new level in college. For those of you who don't recognize the condition, here's the definition according to Merriam-Webster's (2003):

> To put off intentionally and habitually
> To put off intentionally the doing of something that should have been done

That probably sounds familiar. And all of those brutally serious definitions have consequences. When you put off homework, bills, or a job, you are setting aside the stuff that matters for things that don't matter, like going to the mall, watching TV, or just being lazy.

Let's talk about each part of the definition: *To put off intentionally and habitually.* Surely, you don't purposely put off your work, do you? There's always a reason, whatever it may be.

Sorry. Procrastination is intentional, whether you're ready to admit it or not. And it can become an insidious little habit, a way of living. After all, when you put off homework, who's to say that you won't be putting off cleaning your room, washing your car, and calling your grandmother? Fortunately, it is a habit that can be broken through willpower, guidance, and an ability to control what you're thinking.

Now, let's talk about the next part of the definition: To postpone. *Postpone* is a very comforting term. After all, when you postpone, you're only *putting off* something important. You know it has to be done, but yet you don't rush to do it. Why? Because you've postponed it, saying to yourself, "Hey, I just don't feel like it right now."

And now for the last part of the definition: *To put off doing something that should have been done.* Let's face it, when you procrastinate, how often is it for a valid reason? If there were a valid reason, you wouldn't be procrastinating; you'd be focusing on something equally or more important. That isn't procrastination; that's just deciding what is important. If you have a major test coming up that you'd forgotten about and you decide to study for it rather than read your American Politics text for a lecture two days later, that is just time management . . . not procrastination.

Procrastination would be putting down your English text and picking up something that won't benefit your future, like a video game, the TV remote control, or a gossip magazine. When you choose a recreational option, you aren't working on something else important; you're just putting off what is really necessary.

On the other hand, what *is* necessary? If you've said yes to every party invitation and every offer from social clubs for the past month, maybe it's time to practice saying no. Saying no to diversions is a great strategy for managing time and the tendency we all have to procrastinate.

How to Wake Up & Stay Up

Being organized for a day starts in the morning, and waking up can be a problem for anyone. It seems that science is not on your side. Research (Carskadon 1999) has confirmed that a teenager's normal waking hours are from something like ten in the morning till midnight. It might be tough rising at seven to make breakfast after a late night, so here are some tips to get yourself out of bed and moving:

1. Put the alarm away from your bed—way away. No, not under your bed—more like across the room. Let's face it, if you got to bed in the wee hours, the snooze button starts to look good, especially when it's within arm's reach. The solution? Put your alarm clock as far away from your bed as possible. This strategy will work for you. You'll already be up and walking, which will make it seem easier to avoid going back to bed. Try positioning your alarm clock right next to your clothes so that you can get dressed as soon as you shut it off. Make sure this clock placement is okay with your roommate, though. After all, the farthest place from your bed could be your roommate's mattress. Find a spot in the room where the alarm will be far away and also won't disturb your roommate.

2. Get wet. Even if you shower at night, a morning shower can do wonders to help you wake up. While you're at it, shave or put on make-up, brush your teeth, and wash your face. By the time you're scrubbed off, you'll want to jump into some clean comfortable clothes and head out the door to show everyone how good you look. Hey, if it's early and you're making an effort, why not?

3. Eat breakfast. Hopefully you remember from chapter 1 that breakfast should be a habit. Sometimes it's tough to walk all the way to the cafeteria, but eating breakfast ensures a good start to the learning day. It's hard enough listening to an early morning lecture on the history of brooding Dutch art, but doing so on an empty stomach will certainly sabotage your effort.

Frank, a communications and political science double major: *When I started college, I had my alarm right next to my bed. On the last day of classes, I had it all the way across the room, on top of my stereo. To turn the alarm off, I would have to get out of bed and shut it off.*

Weekends

The word "weekend" is a synonym for "salvation" in college— no classes, no lectures, no labs. Just two days worth of lounging in front of the television with a fresh box of crackers, right? 'Fraid not. Sure, there is time for chilling, but not the entire weekend. Weekends are by far the best time to catch up on your homework. How can you manage your weekend? Cut out the things that don't matter.

Let's look at a typical Saturday morning:

- Play video games—thirty minutes
- Read a sports magazine—fifteen minutes

- Check e-mail—twenty minutes
- Run to the snack machine—ten minutes
- Call friends on the phone—fifteen minutes

Each of those activities may not seem to take much time, but added together it's a wasted hour and a half! It is amazing how much time is lost when you get distracted by little time wasters like these. Alternatively, you could have planned a longer event that would have been more fun and important.

PLAN YOUR WEEKEND

Record in advance, even if just in your mind, how your Saturday and Sunday will be spent, down to the hour if you choose. Figure out what you're going to do during each portion of the day. It doesn't have to be all work. If you write down "Football game—two hours," then you know you've set aside that portion of the day for the game. And that's great! Relaxation has its place. But it can't be more important than homework. So schedule time to complete your homework, too. Perhaps when the Sunday late-morning news dominates the TV, or maybe when your friends are all at work—whenever it is, make a plan, even if just on the agenda of your mind, and stick to it.

CATCH UP OR EVEN GET AHEAD

Catching up and even getting ahead is what the weekend is really for. It's pretty tough to read ahead seventy-five pages in your Elementary Education Methods textbook on a Tuesday when you have a lot of other assignments to do. But that same chapter can be a piece of cake on a Saturday afternoon. Most college students we surveyed agreed they would have been more successful and less stressed if they had used weekends to their advantage. Fred figured out that he could benefit from using his weekends to catch up and get ahead during his second semester.

REWARD YOURSELF

During the weekend, there will be enticing campus events— maybe a homecoming game, a rock concert, or a fraternity touch football game. Unfortunately, if you decide that you'd rather go to all of those than study for a possible Biochemistry pop quiz, you're going to be hurting when Monday morning comes around. The best way to get it all done? Plan your weekend around one splashy event and then look forward to it as a reward. If you don't want to study for your quiz on Saturday night, then go to the concert that night and dedicate yourself to studying on Sunday. Or decide to use some reward time simply to be idle. Sit on a bench. Linger over an espresso. Call your favorite uncle. Weekends are for the precious little things that get lost during the week. You will enjoy them so much more if you have a plan and know that you are on top of the things that are important to you.

WRITE IT DOWN

Jotting down notes, whether on a computer to-do list, sticky notes, or a page in your datebook, gets your brain doing more than just thinking about it. The notes feed action. Think of the writing as fuel—when you write something down, it gives your brain some gas to go to work! Hey, it worked for Albert Einstein, who is said to have always carried a pencil and paper with him no matter where he was. Writing reminders for yourself can be a part of your lifestyle of being organized. For example, do you love to shop? If your room is becoming full of clothes that you hadn't planned on buying, maybe you should make a list before you go to the sale at the mall. Writing a list will help you avoid impulsive purchases and instead enjoy the possessions you already own.

MAKE IT A GROUP ACTIVITY

Homework assignments aren't what most students would naturally prefer to do on the weekend. The good news is that you can band together with some of your friends to cope with this awful truth. Create a study group. Help each other with assignments. Check in on your friends every few hours to make sure they're still studying. Working with a group can offer a welcome break, and you can chill out even if you're still discussing homework. Moral support is good in any situation!

Free Up Your Brain for Learning

College life is filled with assignments, dates, page numbers, and other details that seem like so much minutia. It can be difficult to remember all the things that matter. You are going to have to find the best way to keep track of your life. Now, if you're not that happy clicking on a computer, don't try to organize everything on your laptop. And, vice versa, if you're not a pen and notebook person, writing things down isn't the best choice for you. Here are just a few examples of ways to keep track of your life in college and free up your brain for learning.

Calendar. The old standby. At home, there was probably a calendar on your refrigerator, packed with dates and times and reminders. It was always visible and easy to spot. If you are comfortable using a calendar, who says you need a change? Make sure you mount the calendar someplace in your room where it will be very visible to you, or in a spot that you go to often, like the front door. Have a system for filling it out. Try dividing the day into "responsibilities" and "activities." Doing so will allow you to see what you need to get accomplish, and what you have planned for fun throughout the day.

Dry erase boards. These tools are very nice. Use them to keep track of friends' phone numbers or to count down the days to a big project due date. Dry erase boards are like calendars. They need constant updating. You have to refer to them often. They can be a great tool if you consider yourself a hands-on person. They're also a great way to communicate with friends—by mounting one outside your dorm room door!

Day planner. In high school, you had an assignment book. Maybe you didn't use it because you were afraid of looking nerdy, uncool, or just plain weird. Well, things have changed. It is cool to be smart and organized in college. A day planner is nice because it's easily transportable. You can carry it in your backpack wherever you go. It's there anytime you need to write something down, like "Buy a card for Sis's birthday."

Sticky notes. These sticky pieces of paper can be used for everything that does not fit into a calendar, dry erase board, or notebook. But it can be annoying having a million little pieces of paper flying around your dorm room, so throw them away when you complete something. It is a physical gesture that tells you that a particular job has been completed and can be put out of your mind.

Alarms. Humans generally respond to sound. By setting an alarm, you can define the time available for an activity or a task. Say you're planning to watch TV for forty-five minutes and no longer because you've got an art assignment you have to start. If you're watching something that you really enjoy, it can be tough to put that remote down and pick up your art history book. You might not glance at the clock; you'd rather just get lost in the idea that you're only watching TV for forty-five minutes. An alarm will keep you honest.

Handheld electronic organizers. A handheld electronic organizer can do everything already mentioned . . . and more. They feature calendars, alarms, and assignment sections. They can be used to keep track of phone numbers. They can even send you an alert when you're due on the other side of campus for your work-study job in the admissions office. While they're an expensive organizational tool, for some they will be the most valuable. Many students who use them find themselves more prompt and organized. If you can afford one and feel like it would help you, try it.

Living with a Disorganized Roommate

So, what if you and your roommate qualify as the Odd Couple when it comes to staying organized? What is true about all roommate experiences—good and bad—is that they prepare you for real life. You become more mature working through conflicts, like deciding who is going to throw out those greasy pizza boxes stacked beside the trash can. Most colleges try to match roommates with common interests and lifestyles. In all cases, you must talk with your roommate about your expectations and plans so that both of you can meet your academic goals. If you don't want your roommate having a card game on Wednesday night before your German vocab test on Thursday morning, say so. If you begin to feel like you are living in a pigsty because your roommate's wardrobe is stored in piles on the floor, gather up the nerve to discuss it. Don't allow your stomach to churn and your cheeks to turn red. Just say it calmly: "Can we talk about cleaning up the room?" But flexibility works both ways. Offer to help. Set a time to clean the room together. Thank your roommate for being considerate of your need to feel organized.

Sooner or Later You Will Get Organized

Sometimes it takes a life-altering event to knock a person off a disorganized course and to get back on to the straight and narrow. However you gain organizational awareness—whether it's through an overdraft notice from your bank, an F on a calculus test, or a friend's confrontation about your messy car—this awareness will give you great mental health rewards. The sooner you begin to appreciate the value of organization, the better.

Don't wait for a wake-up call from an emotionally distressing event. The chronic stress of being disorganized, losing important documents, and forgetting important deadlines can ruin your chances of success in college. Living as simply as possible involves unburdening your life and living with fewer distractions —whether they be material things, activities, or relationships. Again, saying no can be the most effective tool you have to stay organized. Another trick is to ask yourself, "Is this activity going to simplify and unclutter my life?" Resign from organizations whose meetings you dread. Learn to live with less information. Stop watching TV news. Cancel half of your e-mail newsletters. Save some of your monthly earnings or spending allowance and learn to live on the rest. It might take a long walk in the park or a drive home to identify all the ways to experience life with fewer distractions.

Where to Find Help

In national surveys, most college students reported satisfaction with their academic experience, though many spend less time studying than faculty recommend. Almost 90 percent of students rate their college experience as good or excellent, according to the National Survey of

Student Engagement (2004), a survey of students at over six hundred universities. In spite of this positive rating, researchers also reported that only a small proportion of students interacted individually with their teachers. In fact, in this survey, many students cited little or no interaction with their professors outside of class time. The implication of this study's findings is that students need to visit with their professors and seek out academic assistance before they feel overwhelmed by the stress of keeping up in college.

Many tools and strategies exist to help students. Getting connected with the help that is right for you—before it is too late—is the key. You may find just the help you need online. Visit www.ulife.com. This site offers college students a section called Homework Helper. Check out this link to a whole community of academicians who are available to help with homework questions.

Even though your first year at college is full of challenges, many of the strategies you have read about in this book will surely help you. Remember, your new independence gives you endless opportunities to try out the survival skills in this book. In the end, you will find it really is possible to stay fit and excel during your first year of college. Fred did it, and you will too.

finding help

Eating Healthy

There are Web sites with good diet advice designed to help you reach your weight-loss goals. If you are comfortable using the computer to find answers to your diet questions, consider the following sites.

All about nutrition: www.eatright.org is the American Dietetic Association's Web site and features a variety of tools and online brochures designed to help you make wise dining choices.

Tailoring a diet: www.eDiets.com is the most visited health, fitness, and nutrition site on the Web. It lets you tailor a diet based on how much weight you want to lose and the type of diet you are willing to consider. By typing in your information you receive a food plan (for a fee) tailored to your needs.

Daily goals: www.fitday.com provides a free Web-based journal where you can type in your food intake, weight loss, and fitness goals and have it presented back to you in a graph. A small fee is required for software that features more advanced tracking tools.

Motivational tips: www.ivillage.com/diet is a site with dozens of articles covering diet plans, how to break bad habits, motivational tips, and fitness programs and tips.

Keeping Fit

If sitting at the computer sounds like a way to get started with fitness, that's okay. There are Web sites that will help you find the type of exercise that's right for you.

Walking: Walking builds endurance and burns fat, and you can get started at www.walking.about.com, www.emedicinehealth. com, or www.suite1010.com.

Running: There are three Web sites we have found that give you everything you need to get started, from programs for beginners to race training, race schedules, injury prevention tips, and running gear recommendations. These are: www.runningplanet.com, www.runner sworld.com and www.running page.com.

Yoga: If you have a mat and some soothing music, you can begin yoga by visiting www.yoga.com, www.yogabasics.com, or www.yogadirectory.com.

Pilates: Similar to yoga, this practice improves flexibility and strength. Get started by visiting www.exercise.about.com, www.pilates-studio. com, or www.pilatesmethodalliance.org.

Aerobics: To improve cardiovascular fitness, an aerobic routine may be the answer. Check out www.webaerobics.com, www.turn step.com, or www.aboutaerobics.com.

Strength Building

Weight lifting: You might want to read the American College of Sports Medicine's position statement on weight lifting. You will find the latest literature on weight lifting as well as suggested training guidelines at www.acsm-msse.org.

Personalize your workout: www.ExRx.net is a comprehensive weight lifting site with exercises for beginners and those who are ready for the Olympics. The site has interesting illustrations of the skeletal and muscle systems and ways to personalize a workout.

Health Tests

Dr. Smith (Fred's dad) recommends the following tests for college students:

- General check-up—once annually
- Vision exam—once initially after the age of twenty and then follow-up exams at the direction of your health care provider
- Hearing exam—once initially after the age of eighteen
- Dental exam—once annually
- Breast self-exam—monthly
- Pap test/pelvic exam—every one to three years if sexually active or older than age twenty-two
- Chlamydia test—yearly if sexually active
- STD tests—ask your doctor
- Blood pressure test—start at age twenty-one, then annually
- Rectal exam—ask your doctor
- Self-exam for skin disorders—monthly

- Flu vaccine—ask your doctor
- Tetanus-diphtheria vaccine—every ten years
- Meningitis vaccine—recommended for college students at age eighteen or before they begin classes

Medical Kit for the Dorm

Dr. Smith believes that the most common illnesses in the college-age population are colds and sore throats. Many times you can treat these minor afflictions yourself and avoid the hassle of waiting in line at the health service. But if symptoms do not improve with treatment in a few days, then it is time to seek professional advice. Sinus infections and bronchitis are also common, and antibiotic therapy may be required. To avoid common viral infections from the get-go, wash your hands often, get plenty of rest, and eat fruits and vegetables. Here is what to have in your medical kit.

- Ibuprofen
- Sudafed or Tylenol Cold
- Cough drops
- Thermometer
- Imodium
- Metamucil
- Disposable rubber gloves
- A variety of sizes of bandages
- A washcloth to be used as a compress
- Rubbing alcohol

To treat colds: Plan for as much extra sleep as you can. May take two (200 mg) ibuprofen every four hours. Drink lots of water. If you experience congestion, take Sudafed or Tylenol Cold.

To treat sore throats: Use cough drops for pain relief, take two (200 mg) ibuprofen every four hours, and drink plenty of orange juice.

To treat chills: If your temperature is 100 degrees or above, you have a fever. Take two (500 mg) Tylenol. If your fever spikes to 102 degrees and does not subside with Tylenol, go to the student health services office.

To treat diarrhea: Take two Imodium for the first dose, then one with each loose stool up to a maximum of six a day.

To treat constipation: Use Metamucil as directed. Wait for results. The most common cause of constipation is lack of water and fiber in the diet. Choose a bran cereal every morning. Drink water while studying.

To treat cuts: Always wear gloves when someone else's blood is present. Use soap and water, or alcohol, to clean cuts. Apply pressure until the bleeding stops, then bandage. If necessary, use a clean washcloth to apply pressure for abrasions with large blood loss. Afterward, soak the cloth in cold water, then launder in hot water.

To treat sprains and strains: Take two (200 mg) ibuprofen every four hours. Apply ice to bruises, bumps, strains, and sprained areas.

VISITING THE HEALTH SERVICES OFFICE

Find the health services office when you arrive on campus. It will be easier to locate it, usually in the back of an older campus building, when you are feeling well, rather than when you are nauseated or in pain. Usually these offices offer comprehensive outpatient care to meet the most basic health needs of students. Serious or involved medical problems are generally referred to off-campus facilities.

Know your rights as a patient:

- Access to care and treatment regardless of race, creed, sex, origin, or sexual orientation

- Consideration and respect for personal dignity and privacy
- Knowledge of the health care provider's identity
- Expectation that your diagnosis, prognosis, and methods of treatment will be explained clearly
- Clear explanations of your medicines, including the risks and possible side effects
- Your right to refuse treatment
- Your right to request a copy of your bill

Your responsibilities as a patient:
- Provision of your best knowledge and accurate information related to the health matter
- Following the treatment plan
- Acceptance of personal responsibility if you refuse treatment
- Assumption of financial obligation for the services received (carry your insurance card with you)
- Respect for rights of other patients and office personnel

Your college health service may offer the following basic services:
- Nursing assessment
- Birth control
- Laboratory tests
- Orthopedic appliances and dressings as ordered by the physician
- Mental health referrals
- Pregnancy testing
- Sports injury assessment
- Substance abuse counseling
- Sexually transmitted disease testing

The following treatment and prevention services may also be available:

- Allergy injections
- Excision of lesions
- Gynecological exams
- Immunizations
- Massage therapy
- Pharmacy
- Routine physical examination by a physician
- Wart removal

ACCIDENT & SICKNESS INSURANCE

If you are not covered under a family insurance plan, your college may offer a nonrenewable accident and sickness insurance policy to use while you are attending college. This is usually inexpensive. It may be billed through the college. Inquire at your student services office or the health services office.

In most cases, an insurance plan will cover only services from authorized providers. If you need to see a specialist or someone who is outside of your provider group, you will have to complete a referral authorization. Don't be dismayed by the processes and paperwork involved with health care today. It's a necessary part of your effort to get well.

bibliography

American Academy of Family Physicians, American Academy of Pediatrics, American School Counselor Association, et al. 2004. Experts agree that marijuana and learning don't add up. *USA Today*, Oct. 26, 10A.

American Dietetic Association. 1992. *Eating Well the Vegetarian Way*. Chicago, Ill.: The American Dietetic Association.

———. 1994. *Water: The Beverage for Life*. Chicago, Ill.: The American Dietetic Association.

———.1997. *Safe Eating: A Guide to Preventing Foodborne Illness*.

———. 2002. Total diet approach to communicating food and nutrition information. *Journal of the American Dietetic Association* 102:100.

Beecher, L. H. 2004. Medications for depression. *Minnesota Health Care News*, July 1.

Carper, J. 2005. Five reasons to eat yogurt. *USA Weekend*, Jan. 21, 4.

Cull, J. 2003. *Food for Life*. Minnetonka, Minn.: National Health and Wellness Club.

Des Moines Sunday Register. 2004. *College Guide 2004-05*.

Dubuque Telegraph Herald. 2005. Study: Simple activity keys weight loss. Jan. 29, 6A.

Duyff, R. 1996. *The American Dietetic Association's Complete Food and Nutrition Guide.* Minnetonka, Minn.: Chronimed Publishing.

Edwards, P., and S. Edwards. 1994. *Working from Home.* New York: Penguin Putnam Publishing.

Hellmich, N. 2004. Sleep loss may equal weight gain. *USA Today*, Dec. 7, 1D.

Landgraf, G. 1999. Behind the buzz: What every student should know about caffeine. *UTD Digital Mercury* 19(28). Accessed March 7, 2006, at http://mercury.utdallas.edu/old/1999/v19n28/ buzz.html.

Ma, Y., E. R. Bertone, E. J. Stanek III, et al. 2003. Association between eating patterns and obesity in a free-living US adult population. *American Journal of Epidemiology* 158(1):85-92.

Marlein, M. B. 2002. College students satisfied, but they need to study more. *USA Today*, Nov. 12, 7D.

McGinn, D., and R. Depasquale. 2004. Taking depression on. *Newsweek*, Aug. 23, 59.

Medline Plus. 2004. www.nlm.nih.gov/medlineplus/exerciseandphysical fitness.html

Monahan, K. 2004. Brain trust. *Today's Health and Wellness*, Jan., 62.

National Center for Chronic Disease Prevention and Health Promotion. 1999. Physical activity and health: A report of the surgeon general. At-a-glance. www.cdc.gov/nccdphp/sgr/ata glan.htm.

National Center for Nutrition and Dietetics. 1997. Straight answers about vitamin and mineral supplements.

National Institute of Mental Health. 1999. Depression research at the National Institute of Mental Health. Accessed March 7, 2006, at www.nimh.nih.gov/publicat/depresfact.cfm.

Osterweil, N. 2000. Thanks for the memories? Sleep may deserve some credit. WebMD. Accessed March 7, 2006, at http://my.webmd.com/ content/article/26/1728_59518.htm?lastselectedguid=(5FE84E90-BC 77-4056-A91C-9531713 CA348}

Reno Gazette-Journal. 2004. Sleep problems can add pounds. Nov. 16, 1.

Somer, E. 2001. *The Origin Diet.* New York: Henry Holt Publishers.

The Lutheran. 2005. Study: Religion can ease college stress. Jan. 9.

Walsleben, J., and R. Baron Faust. 2001. *A Woman's Guide to Sleep.* New York: Three Rivers Press.

Westcott, W. Massachusetts Governor's Committee on Physical Fitness and Sports. *Start swimming.* www.govfitness.com/swimming.html.

references

Ainsworth, B. E., W. L. Haskell, A. S. Leon, et al. 1993. Compendium of physical activities: Classification of energy costs of human physical activities. *Medicine and Science in Sports and Exercise* 25(1):71-80.

Allison, K. C., and L. S. Friedman. 2004. Digestion: Soothing a sensitive gut. *Newsweek*, Sept. 27, 47.

American Dietetic Association. 1997. *Disordered Eating and Eating Disorders*. Chicago, Ill.: The American Dietetic Association.

American Dietetic Association Foundation. 1995. *Migraine Headaches and Food*. Accessed March 7, 2006, at www.myparentime.com/articles/articleS134.shtml.

American Heart Association. 2003. Eating breakfast may stave off obesity, diabetes. 43rd annual conference of the American Heart Association, March 6.

American Music Therapy Association, 2006. What is music therapy? http://www.musictherapy.org.

Associated Press. 2004. Study confirms sleep essential for creativity. Accessed March 7, 2006, at www.cnn.com/2004/HEALTH/01/21/sleep.creativity.ap/.

Benson, H., and J. Corliss. 2004. Relaxation: Ways to calm your mind. *Newsweek*, Sept. 27, 47.

Boreham, C. A. G., R. A. Kennedy, M. H. Murphy, et al. 2005. Training effects of short bouts of stair climbing on cardiorespiratory fitness, blood lipids, and homocysteine in sedentary young women. *British Journal of Sports Medicine* 39(9):590-593.

Califano, J. 2004. National Survey on Drug Use and Health Results. Rockville, MD: SAMHSA, Office of Applied Studies. 4.

Carskadon, M. 1999. When Worlds Collide: Adolescent Need for Sleep Versus Societal Demands, *Adolescent Sleep Needs and School Starting Times*, Phi Delta Kappa Educational Foundation.

Chakravarthy, M. V., M. J. Joyner, and F. W. Booth. 2002. An obligation for primary care physicians to prescribe physical activity to sedentary patients to reduce the risk of chronic health conditions. *Mayo Clinic Proceedings* 77(2):165.

Cleveland Clinic Foundation. 2005. Do I have depression? Accessed March 12, 2006, at www.clevelandclinic.org/health/health-info/docs/2200/2276.asp?index=9314&src= news.

Consumer Reports. 2003. Caffeine: Where is it hiding? July.

Depression Health Center. Depression Quiz. http://www.webmd.com/ diseases_and_conditions/depression.htm

Depression and Bipolar Support Alliance. Mental Health Screening Center. http://www.dbsalliance.org/survey

Herbold, N., I. M. Vazquez, E. Goodman, et al. 2004. Vitamin, mineral, herbal and other supplement use by adolescents. *Topics in Clinical Nutrition* 19(4):266-271.

Hill, J. 2003. *Colorado Physical Activity and Nutrition State Plan 2010*, Colorado Department of Health and Environment, 20.

Hoffmann, C. 2004. Personal communication.

Hofius, S. 2004. Study: Spiritually inclined students happier. *Asbury Park Press*, Nov. 2, 15.

Howarth, N. C., T. T. Huang, S. B. Roberts, et al. 2005. Dietary fiber and fat are associated with excess weight in young and middle-aged U.S. adults. *Journal of the American Dietetic Association* 105(9):1365-1372.

Jackson, K. 2005. Exercise abuse—Too much of a good thing. *Today's Dietitian* 7(3):51.

Kantrowitz, B. 2004. What dreams are made of. *Newsweek*, Aug. 9, 41.

Kelly, W. 2004. Personal communication.

Kilgore, C. 2000. Creatine and andro popular among high school athletes. *Family Practice News* 30(11):22.

Kindler, D. 2004. Dangers of college sleep deprivation. http://journalism. nyu.edu/pubzone/livewire/000114.php.

Kleinman, R. E., S. Hall, H. Green, et al. 2002. Diet, breakfast, and academic performance in children. *Annals of Nutrition and Metabolism* 46 (Suppl. 1):24-30.

Lang, S. 2003. CU nutritionists: Junk food, all-you-can-eat make "freshman 15" a reality. *Cornell Chronicle*, Aug. 28. Accessed March 7, 2006, at www.news.cornell.edu/Chronicle/03/8.28.03/ freshman_15.html.

Levitsky, D., and T. Youn. 2004. The more food young adults are served, the more they overeat. *Journal of Nutrition* 134:2546-2549.

Lewis, J., and J. Adler. 2004. Forgive and let live. *Newsweek*, Sept. 27, 47.

Marcason, W. 2004. What do "net carb," "low carb," and "impact carb" really mean on food labels? *Journal of the American Dietetic Association*, 104(1):135.

Mayo Clinic Staff. 2004. Stretches you can do in the office. Mayo Foundation for Medical Education and Research. Accessed March 7, 2006, at www.mayoclinic.com/health/stretching/ WL00030.

Mayo Clinic Staff. 2005a. Adolescent sleep problems. Mayo Foundation for Medical Education and Research. Accessed March 7, 2006, at www.mayoclinic.com/health/teens-health/CC00019.

———. 2005b. Core exercises: Beyond your average abs routine. Mayo Foundation for Medical Education and Research. Accessed March 7, 2006, at www.mayoclinic. com/health/core-exercises/SM00071.

Merriam-Webster. *Merriam-Webster's Collegiate Dictionary.* 11th edition. 2003. Springfield, Mass.: Merriam-Webster.

Milius, R. 2004. Personal communication.

National Institute of Allergy and Infectious Diseases (NIAID). 2005. Facts and Figures. Allergy Statistics. U.S. Department of Health and Human Services: National Institutes of Health, August. 1.

NAASO. 2004. Lack of sleep may lead to excess weight (press release). NAASO, the Obesity Society. Accessed March 12, 2006, at www.naaso.org/news/20041116.asp.

National Survey of Student Engagement. 2004. *Student Engagement Pathways to Collegiate Success.* Bloomington, Ind.: National Survey of Student Engagement.

Pfeiffer, T. 1997. "Zombified" students roam residence halls. Drake University School of Journalism and Mass Communications Cyberpress. Accessed March 7, 2006 at www.drake.edu/cyberpress/2-25/zombies.html.

Pope, H., and D. Yurgelun-Todd. 1996. The residual cognitive effects of heavy marijuana use in college students. *Journal of the American Medical Association* 275(7):521-527.

Rampersaud, G., M. A. Pereira, B. L, Girard, et al. 2005. Breakfast habits, nutritional status, body weight, and academic performance in children and adolescents. *Journal of the American Dietetic Association* 105(5):743-760.

Rennard, B., R. F. Ertl, and G. F. Gossman. 2000. Chicken soup inhibits neutrophil chemotaxis in vitro. *Chest* 118:1150-1157.

Rolls, B. 2004. Have a salad before you start. *Medical News Today*, Oct. 5. Accessed March 7, 2006, at www.medicalnewstoday.com/medical news.php?newsid=14495.

Schoon, A. 2004. More students are seeking help from UI psychologists. *The University of Iowa FYI*, Sept. 3, 4.

Sharp, L. 2002. Screening for depression across the lifespan. *American Journal of Family Practice* 66: 1001.

Shapira, N., M. C. Lessig, T. D. Goldsmith, et al. 2003. Problematic Internet use. *Depression and Anxiety* 17:201-216.

Sorgen, C. 2003. Want to lose weight? Get some sleep. WebMD. Accessed March 7, 2006, at http://my.webmd.com/content/article/61/71413.htm?lastselectedguid={5FE84E90-BC77-4056-A91C-95317 13CA348}.

Spiegel, K., E. Tasali, P. Penev, et al. 2004. Brief communication: Sleep curtailment in healthy young men is associated with decreased leptin levels, elevated ghrelin levels, and increased hunger and appetite. *Annals of Internal Medicine* 141(11):846-850.

Spilner, M. 2001. Walking fit. *Prevention*, June, 95-96.

Springen, K. 2004. Women, cigarettes, and death. *Newsweek*, May 10, 69.

Stabile, L. 2005. Combined targeting of the estrogen receptor. *Cancer Research* 65:1459.

Taheri, S., L. Lin, D. Austin, et al. 2004. Short sleep duration is associated with reduced leptin, elevated ghrelin, and increased body mass index. *Public Library of Science* 1(3):e62. Accessed March 7, 2006, at www.pubmedcentral.nih.gov/articlerender.fcgi?artid=535 701.

Twersky, O. 2000. From Z's to A's: Teens need more sleep. WebMD. Accessed March 7, 2006, at http://my.webmd.com/ content/article/28/1728_61805.htm?lastselectedguid={5FE84E 90-BC77-4056-A9 1C-9531713CA3480

Twohill, G. 2004. Personal communication.

Wurtman, R. J. 1995. Brain serotonin, carbohydrate-craving, obesity and depression. *Obesity Research* 3:477S-480S.

Zakay-Rones, Z., N. Varsano, M. Zlotnick, et al. 1995. Inhibition of several strains of influenza virus in vitro and reduction of symptoms by an elderberry extract (*Sambucus nigra L.*) during an outbreak of influenza B Panama. *Journal of Alternative and Complementary Medicine* 1(4):361-369.

Zemel, M. B., W. Thompson, A. Milstead, et al. 2004. Calcium and dairy acceleration of weight and fat loss during energy restriction in obese adults. *Obesity Research* 12(4):582-590.

M.J. Smith, RD, FADA, is a registered dietitian and fellow of the American Dietetic Association. She is licensed to practice dietetics in Iowa and has spent twenty years teaching families how to make food choices to manage disease and foster daily vitality. She has written twelve books about nutrition and health, which together have sold more than 400,000 copies. Her book *Diabetic Low Fat and No-Fat Meals in Minutes* won a National Health and Wellness Bronze Award from the National Health Information Awards Program. Another, *Brand Name Low Fat Meals in Minutes*, was a Doubleday Book Club selection and sold more than 100,000 copies. Smith's work has appeared in **USA Today, Good Housekeeping, Shape, Ladies Home Journal, Essence, Good Taste, Diabetes in the News, The Lutheran, Today's Health and Wellness** and many health and Midwest regional publications.

Fred Smith graduated with honors in 2003 from Clayton Ridge High School. He served as president of the student body. During high school, he participated in choral and instrumental music, speech, drama and golf. Fred is going to be a senior at Luther College in Decorah, IA and has a double major in communications and political science.